Art Nouveau
in France

ART NOUVEAU

in France

Jean-Paul Midant

Books & Co.

We would like to thank the following persons for their help in the preparation of this book: Bertrand Fleury, Caroline Mierop, Patricia Pedraccini, Béatrice Salmon, Françoise Sylvestre, Valérie Thomas, William Wheeler,   Galerie Fournier,   Galerie Impulsion B.,   Galerie Giovanni,   Galerie J-Point.

Translated by William Wheeler
© L'Aventurine, Paris, 1999.
© Media Serges/Books & Co., Paris, 1999.
ISBN 2-84509-102-8

Foreword

At the end of the 19th century numerous artists, exercising their skills in a variety of disciplines, expressed the ardent desire to live and produce in the present, and to do away with the conventions which prevented them from giving full expression to their talents. They joined forces under the banner of Art Nouveau which rallied together in France artists as diverse as Emile Gallé, Eugène Grasset, Hector Guimard and Victor Prouvé. It is usually caricatured as the umpteenth battle in the ongoing war of the styles. And a battle which is usually considered as taking place only in the fields of decorative arts. Can the intellectual effervescence of the 1890's and the 1900's be limited to the struggle to impose plant design in decoration?

This study retraces the steps of the protagonists of the movement and explores the sources of inspiration of its modernity. The reader will pause at the Art Nouveau house and its interior, where the family unit comes together, then visit the city and the growing consciousness of its esthetic development. The reader will then visit the 1900 Universal Exhibition in Paris, the culminating point for the movement, where different centers of creation converged. The commercial failure of Art Nouveau will also be covered. Despite its promise, the movement didn't seek or didn't choose to seek to satisfy the wants and needs of its potential customers.

Accompanying the images and the explanatory texts are excerpts from publications, most often articles which appeared in newspapers or in specialized art journals. Their role is to set the scene and illustrate the richness and diversity of the debate about art and the role of the artist in French society at the turn of the century.

Writing this book was an act of pleasure. Its only ambition is to arouse the reader's curiosity to go and discover the objects, the paintings, the houses and apartment buildings which are discussed here.

Victor Prouvé. *Portrait of Emile Gallé*, 1892. Musée de l'Ecole de Nancy.

EMILE GALLÉ

Born on May 4, 1846, Emile Gallé is without doubt the key character to understanding the ambitions of Art Nouveau in France and the originality of its esthetics.

A maker of faience, master glassmaker and furniture designer, Gallé was essentially a naturalist. This does not simply mean that he was interested in botany but that his practice was linked to the intellectual movement, called naturalism, which touched all the branches of art at that period. Thus, he became a collegue of writers, poets, painters and sculptors of his time. Like the brothers Jules and Edmond de Goncourt, Emile Gallé was an instructor. He knew how to exalt the public's sensibility, find the exact words, speak sincerely, act with enthusiasm and develop an artistic vocabulary within the domain of the applied arts. A materialist like Emile Zola, Gallé also believed in science and its benefits without becoming a rigid positivist. As a Republican, he fought against all the excessive and exclusive political ideals which flared up in France at the end of the 19th century and forced the parliamentary regime to fight bitterly for its survival. Severe in his judgement of the modern style, which he considered insubstantial and without a future, he deemed that the study of natural simplicity and logic as well as decoration inspired by plants, was a possible way to regenerate art industries.

Victor Prouvé painted his portrait in the last months of 1892, when Gallé's career was at a crossroad and he was becoming more experimental. His works aroused attention at the technological exhibition of clay, stone and glass which took place in Paris in 1884 organized by the Union Centrale des Arts Décoratifs. By the 1889 Universal Exhibition he was celebrated; remaining obstinately faithful to Nancy, he nonetheless collaborated a short time later with the great socialite Robert de Montesquiou, who gave him access to the most refined circles of the capital.

Marquetry top of *Poppy table*. Marquetry of dahlias and butterflies, 1896. Musée de l'Ecole de Nancy.

Studio of Emile Gallé. *Flower study*. Musée d'Orsay, Paris.

Abandoning ceramics at that point, he took up glasswork and brought to it a natural, symbolical evocation. He notably produced some of his famous poem-vases in which he combined literary themes, matter and decoration on objects that one would imagine as coming from the crust of the earth like spontaneous crystalizations. Thanks to Gallé, the glassmaker shared the quest of the alchemist and the craftsman renewed his experimentation, where science and art became one and the same. The recipe books in which the manufacturer traditionally kept his secrets were replaced by pages annotated with watercolors and hand-written notes next to which poems by Maurice Maeterlinck were copied.

By 1892, Emile Gallé was perfecting the decoration of his furniture, notably with the first masterpieces of marquetry where the reproduction of the local flora of the Lorraine was a recurring theme.

Liberated from academic thinking, open to all sorts of beauty as long as they were as expressive as nature and life, modern man, according to Gallé, created and dreamed of a better world in the presence of what he had created, in a domestic intimacy where research and integrity predominate.

This idealized image espoused by Emile Gallé, living in perpetual enchant-ment, crossing the plains and woods of his native region to discover its secrets, seems far removed from reality. Entrepreneur and man of action, he quickly defended an industrial model which appeared to him to help society evolve

Emile Gallé. *The Wheat* sideboard, 1904, based on a 1903 model. Musée de l'Ecole de Nancy.

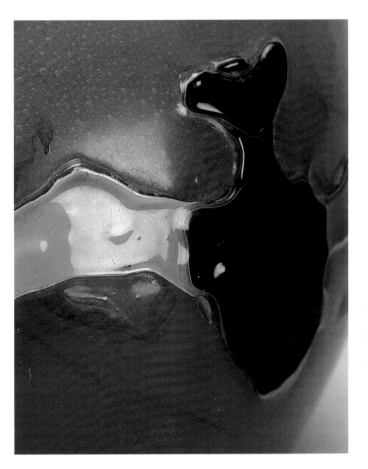

Emile Gallé. Spherical vase with "bat" design and detail. Musée de l'Ecole de Nancy.

towards more justice, driven by a code of generous, communal ethics. Here one could evoke the pursuit of an Anglo-Saxon intellectual attitude, and recognize William Morris's influence, he himself an industrialist, militant socialist and whom several leading figures of European Art Nouveau considered as their leader. The comparaison, however, would make little sense. Gallé's commitment was also political and, from 1890 to the beginning of the new century, went well beyond the simple production of pretty "objets d'art" for a privileged few. He was in favor of the Republic in the troubled climate of the Général Boulanger affair, the Panama Scandal, the Dreyfus affair and the battle for lay education.

Active until his death in 1904, he was the first president of the School of Nancy (Alliance provinciale des industries d'art), a private association founded in February 1901 to develop artistic craft companies in the province of Lorraine. Bringing industrialists, artists and intellectuals together, the School of Nancy proposed classes and lectures in draftsmanship and artistic crafts, organized exhibitions and collected the first works for a decorative arts museum which would function as a conservatory of trade skills.

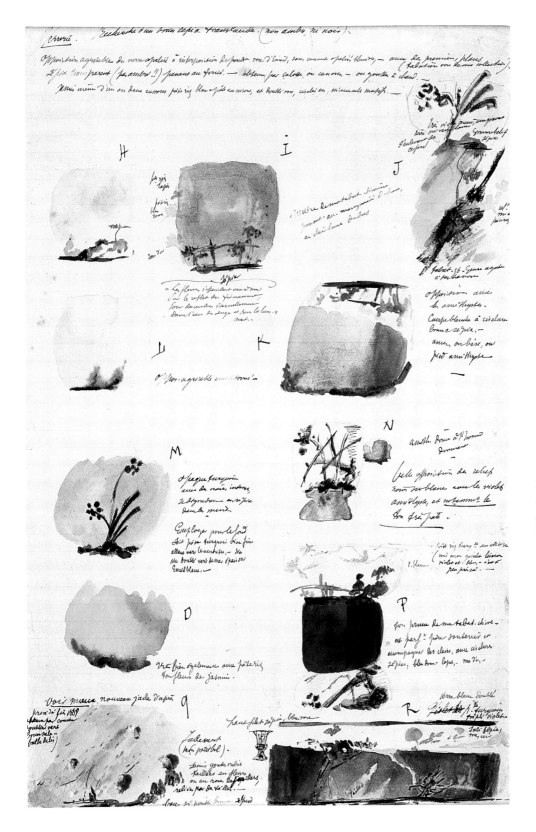

Emile Gallé. Page with samples of sepia tones for glasswork. Musée d'Orsay, Paris.

Emile Gallé. *La Soude* vase, 1903. Executed for the 30th anniversary of the Solvay Company, Dombasle. Musée de l'Ecole de Nancy.

Emile Gallé. Bilobed vase in blond glass with agate effects. Blobs of white crystalized glass, applied while heated, roll down the sides. Private collection.

The Paths of Autumn

Emile Gallé. *Revue des Arts décoratifs,* Paris, 1893, p. 333-335.

The scheme was to construct a credenza outfitted for autumn, a "stand of high vintage and majesty", which could reflect even a concert of instruments, flourishes or muted tones of brass and thanks giving in full festive light.

Sound works always seem to us as though they just sprung spontaneously from the earth, and we believe we hear the harmonious sounds which presided at their birth. Let this present piece appear only as crazed vegetation which has climbed from your floor to your ceiling beams !

Just imagine then that this entire piece would be constructed from the growth of two very ancient vinestocks, sculpted in *young elm*, the brother wood of the vine shoots, in figures of roots and woody stems, of lizards and small insects.

At first, the two stocks hoist themselves above their squat base. They build the bottom of the frame solidly, the subfoundation with the pivoting slots to hold the dishes and slide the silver drawers. Their extensions stretch out to form the border of the well-polished frame of the elm bur top and to hold the mosaic panels in frames and mouldings embellished with vignettes and realistically ringed and cockled bands.

The twin vinestocks, by force of age – we see their stumps racked by winters and human routine – then grow into two towering columns turned in the Champagne region style and tied with willow stems, forming the sides of the cabinet and the supports of the presentation shelves.

From the summit rise the budding spikes of the crest colonettes. Here arches festoon, heavy with snails and ripe bunches of grapes. They come together and entwine at the crowning of the barrel vault, or arbor of fancy goods, which forms a canopy and multicolor pavilion for the whole edifice.

But to speak in modern language, let us say that the sense of decoration in the sideboard lies in the intentional opposition between the rendering of tangible objects and certain visions of lofty things, those remote things which are desired or must be divined.

Look at the ground. The ornament makes contact with our old earth and with the life of the field. Above, the backs of the piece are covered with shadows. The decoration, which is naturalistic here, grows blurred over there and becomes a symbol.

Therefore, in your hands lies the fauna and the herbarium of the vineyard "in the hot season". Here are its special tares, portrayed lifelike in wood mosaics, in August and September colors from the sun spurge to the field calendula. Then the animated guests arrive : warblers, thrushes tipsy from the grape harvest, with the notation of their small bird cries in winged characters, – *tsic, tsic!* – the strident *b'sic...* the morning migrations in scattered flight and the autumnal refrain of the tufted lark : *tuli! tuli!*

But that is only a preliminary harvest of the motifs which accompany the musing. It in turn frees itself from the slight notations taken from the herbs and the animals, on site, and from the hour and the season. Little by little, thanks to the wonders of regulated light, attenuated nuances and contours, the mysterious atmosphere, propitious to loftiness, takes shape.

Thus, on the three back panels the color scale, which is luminous all around, darkens and grows dim with shades of blue gray. The abundance of models and details is simplified, and veers off into twilight tones.

Dull slate-colors run from one panel to the next, over the top of their frames of blond Amboyna wood, while the representation of low horizons under great expanses of sky gives the compositions an almost mystical character.

The bat, nocturnal country policeman, sets chase to the winegrower's enemies, the phylloxera spectres and the April moon.

On the arch and on this old silver entry, a star-catching spider, the symbol of poetic labor, weaves unknown constellations. An ideal vine strews the celestial road with seeds which are heavenly bodies. With the good old poet Montesquiou, it invites man to relish

"...the juices
From the radiant tunnel of the vine arbor of the worlds,
Whose flaming vine shoots never decay".

And the lofty liana suspends its bunches in lights and girandoles : it is Sirius, it is Aldebaran. Or else it scatters them in scintillating astronomic figures : Orion, the Hyades, the distant Pleiades and

"The globes, the vermeil fruit of divine boughs." Victor Hugo

See at last, beyond the completed harvests, the slow, sinuous spiral of bonfires which are dying out, sighs of the annual task. Praise be to God! it is accomplished...

The heavy lands – Inlaid panel. – Ochrous-colored, dull yellow fallow fields. Undistinguished horizons. Bizarre, motley sky. Lazy, white water. In the sunshine the countryside resembles a tapestry. The fleshy, curled bronzed leaves of *Chenopodium bonus-henricus* swoon in the heat of the day. The crimson and episcopal purple stems glisten among the ashdust pink undersides of leaves.

Of the meadowsweet, the winegrowers'weed, the vibrant air leaves only streaked silhouettes. And the choice of this vineyard plant, *good old Henry*, sweet and edible, was a favor to Mr Henri Vasnier, whose forbearance was not unlike the slowness of the infinitely complicated execution.

Saint Martin's Summer – Inlaid panel. – Low horizon, seen from the top of a ruined patch of ground, recovered for cultivation by the weeds of stone masons. The cute shells of the ground cherry, the color of minium, pale lavender and black nightshade, have flowered with poisons and balms, regrets and omissions, and ownerless vineyards. Here and there some aging vine props, leaf shoots, the deadness of an unharvested small bunch, slit open the changing satin sky and the limitless line of the plains.

Bronze and ironwork – In one part of a recent poem by Mr de Montesquiou-Fezensac, my pencil borrowed the text which decorates and inspires some of the drawer liners, some of the ironwork of the panels, drawn with a chasing tool and which I myself patinated. There are bunches of vine flowers where the screws have become leaf and flower buds. A Virginia creeper provided me with the composition for an escutcheon; the bronze is tinged with purple on the stems, then dulls with the pulp of the green mildew, of black or bluish patina. The drawer pulls are stems and leaves of spotted clematis, the fruits are mixed with stars, *"mysterious grapes"*.

Calendula Inlaid panel. – The ripening quickens during the day, but mornings are growing colder. Delay or proceed with the harvest? That is the question : *"The worries of the wines!"*

The fluff of the wood turns the meticulous work of the marqueter into a fog of pastel, like the hillside. In the blur the blotch of a city can be made out. Closer up, the vineyard floats in the mist. The languishing smile of the sun lingers. In jerky flight, gentle butterflies unfurl and close their brief fans of pleated tan, ashgray and light pink gauze.

But one more hoar-frost and our calendulas will bloom no more, between their silver and gold anxious lashs, the brown wink of their last corollas.

The medlar tree, the vineyard in turquoise. – Five panels on the pediment, inlaid with bronzed fruits ; as soon as the leaves redden, they are swept away...

Deilephila – Mosaic panel – *"The friend of twilight"* that is the moth which has a beautiful turtledove coat, painted in myrtle green, and carmine blond. His caterpillar is wild about the flesh of young shoots.

The panel is in holm-oak, this ivory sky with sooty mottles. Would one not say that the feverish undulations of these veins are the throbbing of the temples under the ringing of dreams ?

Clematis vitis-alba – Panel with inlay. – Good folks call this clematis *"white vine"*; the feathery seeds cover the hedges and olds walls with tufts. Barely visible, the sinuous stems glisten and throw down their supreme calixes at the end of the season. Our native woods must be like the undersides of wings to represent that which was so smart in those fluffy balls and now is only chilling melancholy.

October. – Panel with inlay. – Here are the gleaners of the year. October bullies September and steps on its heels, the North wind buries the dead under leaves and prepares a white repose.

The woods of marquetry don bleak livery. The sky drowns itself in streaming water and boredom. the gusts of wind strip and whip... The rain weeps ; the colors run and become mixed with gray. The symbols of life, chelidonium, "larkweed", ends in drab rotting. The bird hastens its departure and, over the shifting Northern and Western winds, turns South...

Yet the worker completes his work. The master resigns himself to let it go. He sadly signs the work.

The Poem-Vases of Emile Gallé

Jules Rais, "Les Salons de 1898" in *L'Est Républicain*, July 7, 1898.

Emilé Gallé. Vase *La Pluie au bassin fait des bulles* inspired by Théophile Gautier, 1889. Musée de l'Ecole de Nancy.

It would be a gross error only to see in Mr Gallé's work a pleasant game of forms and colors and to reproach, as some have done, the "literature" of his vases. One must honestly either reject all his work or not quarrel with the master over the essential combination he blends of literary themes, matter and decoration. Perhaps, through his sense of play, he may have thrown a motto on some small piece which did not appear to be clearly necessary: at least it was witty and the scrupulous artist demonstrated, down to the arrangement of the ingeniously designed characters, his rare understanding of and his constant meticulousness for decorative effect. We must confess our debt to clumsy imitations to our understanding of how this type of inscription was more suitable elsewhere, and in most cases.

The stanza, the line of poetry engraved on the sides, stem or foot of the vase are not superfluous ornamentation. They do not repeat in different signs what matter and technique have already expressed; they are the prime element of the poem which the vase represents, as a theme in relation to a symphony. It is an element whose distinct presentation is all the more indispensable since the use of flora is almost always the lone requisite to evoke human passions and anxieties. With the result that the work remains clear despite its infinite complexity. Here written thought and image once again are placed by the glassmaker in the context of the nature which inspired them. At the same time, executing the aspect of the things themselves, that is the reason for these images and thoughts, the artist translates these appearances using his personal genius and enriches the feeling, the revitalized impression, of new feelings and new impressions…

16

Gallé, the Musician

Jules Meier-Graefe as quoted in *La Lorraine artiste*, Sunday October 18, 1896, pp. 214-215.

One of the undeniable merits of vases from Nancy is that it would scarcely be possible to produce the impression of fabulous splendor with greater mastery. Several of these vases manifest such a princely nobility which literally grips those who gaze at them. They all possess something mysterious, a mystique, and this mystique is not at all by chance. Gallé is a musician and seeks to be one also in his vases, and this note, like a leitmotif, has been adopted by the entire school. This ideal point of view sets the school of Nancy apart in France. While the whole artistic tradition of modern France tightens its grip on nature and seeks to evolve in the direction of purely technical means, here, on the Eastern border of the country, remnants of romanticism have been conserved or have taken shape. Without a doubt, the proximity of Germany, is, in this area, of considerable if not preponderant influence, for one of the saints adored by the community is Richard Wagner, and one of his dearest ambitions is to find the true cup into which the Holy Grail overflowed. Symbols connected with these legends, as well as modernist and symbolist poetry are hollowed out of the glass; the works are dedicated to the composers and poets of France. The glass is blown and engraved in a sort of religious ecstasy. Moreover, I know of whole descriptive passages, mysterious descriptions with which, following the artists'intentions, one must be familiar in order to be able to appreciate fully their vases.

Emile Gallé. Vase inspired by a poem by Marceline Desbordes-Valmore. Musée de l'Ecole de Nancy.

EUGÈNE GRASSET

Eugène Grasset. Original print published in *Art et Décoration*, Paris, 1899.

The Swiss Eugène Grasset was born in Lausanne on May 25, 1845 and set up residence in Paris in 1871. An industrial designer, he first worked for a decorator of upholstery fabric then gradually started receiving varied commissions. He worked as an illustrator for the journal *Le Musée pour Tous* in 1874. He was asked to design the ornamental capitals for a volume of drawings from the Louvre published by Henri de Chennevières in 1882 in which he pastiched the styles of Jacques Callot, Rembrandt and Géricault. Then the next year he produced ornamentation for *Les Quatre Fils Aymon*, a "Carolingian" novel about very noble and very valiant knights. It was printed using a new type of chromotypography invented by the Parisian printer, Charles Gillot. For this quite peculiar commission, which was a landmark in French printing history, Byzantium, the Celts, intricate tracery, plaiting, and foliated scrolls colored in gold, silver and purple evoked medieval evangelistaries. Illustrations hung like a sign, galloped over the text, opened a window in the upper part of the page or spread a street scene across the bottom. His figures showed affinities with those of the English Pre-Raphaelite painters and Walter Crane. Japanese prints provided inspiration for his use of color and his bold transposition of tints as well as his play with framing. Head of the French revival of printed imagery, he was also one of the first to find his niche in the world of advertising. Thanks to him, the 1890's witnessed the birth of the famous *Semeuse*, the Larousse publishing house logo, the font which to this day still bears Grasset's name, commissioned by Peignot Foundry and through his graphic work, notably for the calendars of *La Belle Jardinière* department store, a certain modern style woman, with the same long, flowing hair and inaccessible beauty as those Sandro Botticelli portrayed in his Renaissance works. This type of pale, unobtrusive young woman clothed in a simple, ample robe is to be found in the stained glass window which he designed in collaboration with the Parisian master glassmaker Félix Gaudin for the Paris Chambre de Commerce, as well as in the large decorative plaque of enamelled lava entitled *Harmonie* presented at the Salon National des Beaux-Arts in 1895. As a professor of industrial drawing and decorative

Eugène Grasset in
collaboration with Félix
Gaudin. *Harmonie*. Enamel
on lava plaque, 1893. Musée
d'Orsay, Paris.

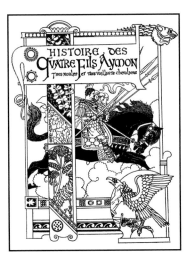

Eugène Grasset. Black proof of the cover of *Quatre Fils Aymon*. Boudet, Paris, 1893.

composition at the Guérin School, a private studio in the Montparnasse district from 1890 to 1903, Grasset jointly published with his students, the most notable of which was Maurice Pillard Verneuil, two volumes of ornamentation which were favorably received by amateurs: *La plante et ses applications ornementales* (1896) and *Méthode de composition ornementale* (1905). His works and articles, which appeared in art journals won over to Art Nouveau, made him an obvious spokesman for the movement but he remained an artist who cared little for naturalism and even less for social activism. In a lecture at the Union Centrale des Arts décoratifs on April 11, 1897, which later appeared in the May and June issues of the *Revue des Arts Décoratifs*, Grasset came out clearly against the realistic school, accused of using unnecessary virtuosity to overcome the difficulties of representing natural objects faithfully. Several lines from the introduction of *Méthode de composition ornementale* show what importance he gave to the senses: "Ornament is born of a desire to use our imagination outside of the pure and simple imitation of natural objects. It is a way of showing our joy of life and comes from a happy state of mind, as if it were the preparation for a party". Grasset's love for geometry, like that for medieval allusions, made him a recognized, respected and original personality, but one with no true followers.

Eugène Grasset. Front and back cover of a school book for Larousse.

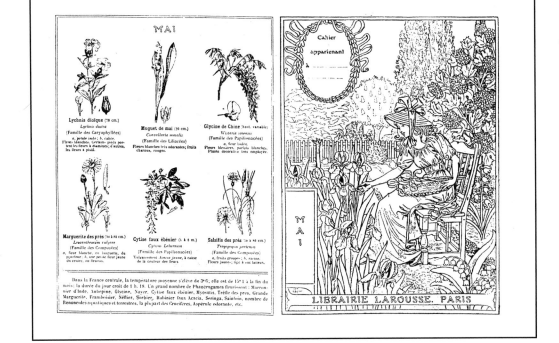

Eugène Grasset. Poster for Larousse. Bibliothèque Forney, Paris.

HECTOR GUIMARD

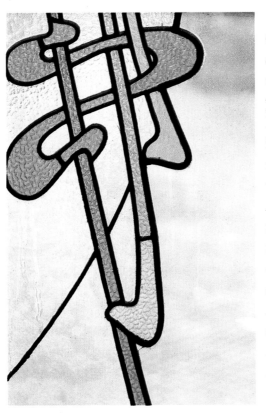

Hector Guimard. *Castel Béranger*, Paris. Detail of stained glass.

Born in Lyon in 1867, Hector Guimard was the youngest of the champions of French Art Nouveau at the turn of the 20th century, twenty years younger than Gallé, Grasset or Prouvé. He enrolled in the new school in Paris, Ecole nationale des arts décoratifs, in 1882 notably with the architect Charles Genuys as his professor. As of 1890 he also served as an instructor at the same school, teaching geometric perspective. His atypical situation of both teacher and student – he was teacher at the above-mentioned institution while studying at the Ecole Nationale des Beaux-Arts for a decade, with mixed results – and his study travels throughout Belgium, Holland, England and Scotland isolated him as a marginal. Then, in 1899, the press (notably *Le Figaro*, which sponsored an exhibition of his work in their salons) and the general public became acquainted with his style upon competition of façades organized by the City of Paris. His entry was curiously named *Castel Béranger*, a block of flats situated in the 16th district in Paris, at 16, rue Lafontaine. Its silhouette owed much to the exceptional architect and archeologist, Eugène Viollet-le-Duc, who had profoundly marked Second Empire architecture in France and was the master designated by the younger generation. The disorderly volume of the building, its asymmetry, the impor-

LE CASTEL BÉRANGER

Pl. 2

Hector Guimard. *Castel Béranger*, Paris. Elevation on rue Lafontaine in *Le Castel Béranger*, Librairie Rouam, 1899.

23

Hector Guimard. Smoking
room banquette, 1897.
Musée d'Orsay, Paris.

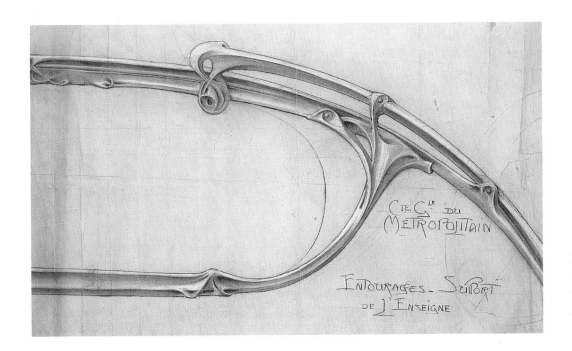

Hector Guimard. Detail of a design for the entrances to the Paris subway. Musée des Arts Décoratifs, Paris.

tance of the upper levels, the frank affirmation of different building materials, were all part of the neo-Gothic vocabulary. However, the layout and decoration of the thirty-six rented flats manifested a distinct, unusual language. Everything was art and art was everywhere. Even favorable critics experienced a certain awkwardness regarding this manifesto, which was only pleasing when considered as a whole. The homogenous style appeared so new that it became bizarre, as the reflection of a lost civilization being reborn in the light. The continual use of the curve in the stylization of plant and animal motifs (to the point of giving the impression that certain pieces of furniture were constructed with bones) generated an uneasiness, as did the presence of strange cast iron anchors locked on the facades and the use of stoneware and glass bricks in the communal areas. This undermined the generous space and light of the living areas and the soft tones used in the color palette. Taking advantage of the enormous curiosity which *Castel Béranger* provoked, several months later Guimard was chosen to design the entrances to the Paris subway lines, which was to become the most visible and most brilliant example in France of this art in the street. This is exactly what the Art Nouveau movement wished to champion.

Hector Guimard. Console
with looking glass frame.
Musée d'Orsay, Paris.

Hector Guimard. Suite of
office furniture, 1909.
Virginia Museum of Fine
Arts, Richmond, Virginia.
Gift of Sydney and Frances
Lewis.

Hector Guimard
Manufacture Nationale de
Sèvres. Two Cerny vases.
The form was created by
Hector Guimard in 1900.
Stoneware with crystalized
glaze. Musée National de
Céramique, Sèvres.

Hector Guimard. Garden
vase and stand. Saint-Dizier
Foundry, 1908. Musée
d'Orsay, Paris.

VICTOR PROUVÉ

Victor Prouvé. *La Soif.*
Bronze vase exhibited at the
Salon National des Beaux-
Arts in 1893, presented to
Admiral Avelan of the
Russian fleet. Present
location unknown.

A native of Nancy, Victor Prouvé was born on August 13, 1858.
He possessed solid training as a painter from his years spent at the
Ecole Nationale des Beaux-Arts in Paris in the early 1880's. A
decade later he became interested in sculpture then pyrogravure.
He would then move on to leatherwork and bookbinding before
turning to murals and teaching.

He was not alone in leaving the lofty domain of art to join the
craftsmen. As of 1891 the Salon National des Beaux-Arts in Paris
exhibited art objects along with painting, sculpture, and (from
1893) architecture; this decision helped promote recognition for
previously discredited and downgraded manual crafts. In an
unprecedented outburst of brotherhood, Pierre Puvis de Cha-
vannes, one of the leading proponents of new school of painting,
exhibited next to the medal engraver Alexandre Charpentier, whose works
demonstrated that he was at ease with pewter as well as with nobler metals.
Sculptors the likes of Auguste Rodin, Jules Dalou and Constantin Meunier
found their works not far from those of the glassmaker Emile Gallé while Paul
Gauguin joined efforts with the potter Ernest Chaplet to produce ceramic
pieces. When these men from different horizons came together at the Salon,
they also exchanged ideas.

For *La Soif,* a small bronze vase presented in 1893, Prouvé had first sculpted
Rubens-like figures in plaster in honor of one of his painting masters. His rendering transformed a fairly common bottle into a flagon brimming over with
vitality and a manifesto for a new-found freedom. With *La Nuit,* exhibited at
the 1895 Salon, he fell closer to the ardor of a Rodin or more specifically to a
Camille Claudel. In her extremely long, wind-swept head of hair, a woman har-
bors owls, bats, several poppies and a crescent moon. She displays apparent
calm in the presence of the tumultuous passions she shelters or provokes. Violent desires are played out by entwined bodies while others agonize: a whole
world of human suffering is stirring. *La Nuit* was a tribute to instinctive nature,

a glorification of the brute beast, echoing the worlds portrayed by Gustave Flaubert, Guy de Maupassant or Octave Mirbeau. Prouvé delighted in matter, as he did in life in general, with unfailing generosity. He was, however, to demonstrate the full measure of his talent and commitment in another art field, in the large murals he produced for the Nancy City Hall (installed in 1892) and later for the City Hall of the suburban Paris town of Issy-les-Moulineaux

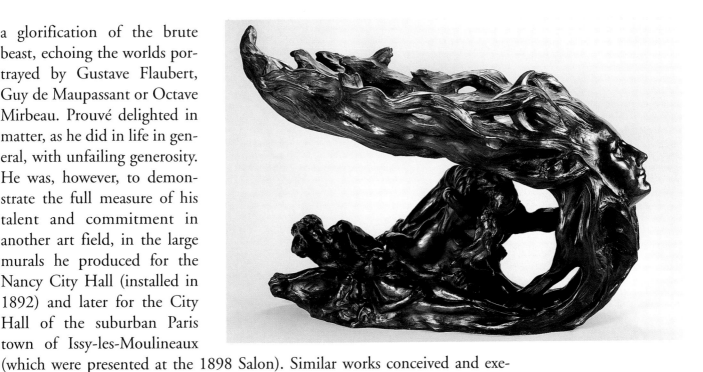

Victor Prouvé. *La Nuit*. Bronze cup exhibited at the Salon National des Beaux-Arts in 1895. Musée de l'Ecole de Nancy.

(which were presented at the 1898 Salon). Similar works conceived and executed between 1899 and 1907 would grace Paris' 11th district town hall.

Victor Prouvé chose to distance himself from his fellow artists with Beaux Arts training and the highly-favored republican allergories of naturalist inspiration. He sought, however, to accentuate and modernize the message of concord of the democratic and republican society he defended and which had been menaced by the political agitation fostered in France between 1890 and 1900. Guided by Eugène Carrière's painting, he moved toward a larger, more lofty, more universal view of humanity. With Albert Besnard Prouvé renewed his color scale, bringing in striking blues and yellows. The artist realized he could add great relief and vitality to rustic scenes while interpreting the beauty of the present. *La Joie de vivre*, a large canvas of 2.6 x 5 meters presented in the grand foyer of the Exposition des Arts Décoratifs in Nancy in 1904 reflected the message conveyed by Art Nouveau for a modern society. Based on work, love of the nurturing earth, sharing and peace, the message appeared in all its manifest simplicity, without breach of continuity, like a vision in the midst of the real world. Men and women embraced their children guided lovingly by grandparents grandchildren toward the waiting arms of their parents. The joyous expectations of the future didn't exclude the uneasiness brought on by thoughts of the past.

Victor Prouvé. *La Joie de vivre*. Canvas presented at the Exposition des Arts Décoratifs in Nancy in 1904. Musée des Beaux-Arts, Nancy.

THE PLANT

Love the plant, not only its stems, leaves and flowers but its flesh, marrow and forceful mass. Draw it. Define its character, transform and stylize it; design an ornament from a blade of grass. Find the fold, the crease, the accent, the curve and by the laws of repetition, softening, or exaggeration, adapt the character of the work to suit the spirit of the plant. Generate a form as found in nature, and, as in nature, find a suitable decor for it. Reflect, progress...

Such was no doubt the ornamenter's creed according to Emile Gallé. It contained numerous original points. Since the factories of the Ancien Régime, the artists, whether they be independent or directly employed by a manufacturer, reproduced popular stock motifs without seeking to modify them. Some of the designers put their heart into their work; others didn't. Through his passionate interest in botany, much like a scientist, Gallé instigated a parallel between experimentation and creation. The studio became a laboratory. Science provided method, design and critical analysis.

The designer began to relate decoration and form. This was a very important factor. Showing concern for design continuity in the transition from a two-dimensional drawing to its three-dimensional materialization and relating intellectual and manual activity was quite uncommon in industrial circles. The independant ceramists, Jean Carriès, Ernest Chaplet and Auguste Delaherche, led the way. In their search to rediscover Far Eastern art, they had

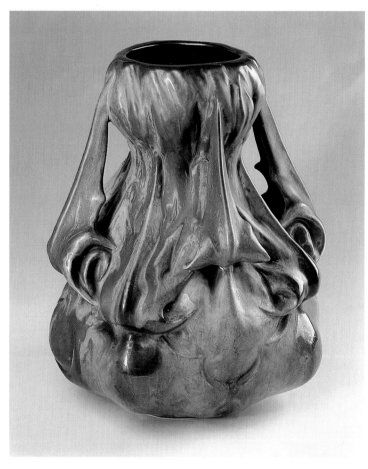

Ernest Bussière. Stoneware vase for Keller and Guérin Company in Lunéville, 1899. Musée de l'Ecole de Nancy.

Previous page: Wisteria and peonies. Embroidery on plush. Charles Fridrich, publisher in Nancy, c. 1900. Musée de l'Ecole de Nancy.

Maurice Pillard Verneuil. Gourds. *Etude de la plante et ses applications aux industries d'art.* Paris, 1908.

Following page:
Sèvres National Manufactory. A pair of Argenteuil vases. The form was created by Henri Barberis in 1897. The sage decoration by Gustave Vignol after Geneviève Rault, 1905. Musée National de Céramique, Sèvres.

established a close relation between thought and matter. This transformation would be even more obvious for master glassmakers, keeping watch over their kilns.

Studying the plant and adopting it as the principal source of inspiration for a new design style provided a means of breaking with current convention without severing ties with tradition. In all the different fields of art, in all cultures and throughout history, plants had served as a primary model, providing form and color. Through its consecutive interpretations by architects, painters, ceramists, weavers, goldsmiths and glassmakers, the plant had become a grammar with specific rules. The plant was present in the Louis XV, Louis XVI and Henri II styles still produced for dining and sitting rooms; it was likewise present in art objets. Yet nonetheless terribly neglected. Couldn't something be done to free it from the past?

This return to the origins of decoration was interpreted by craftsmen in various manners. Liberated from the constraints of the former styles, some were guided by a fascination for technical virtuosity; others viewed it as an ascesis, a newly-discovered simplicity, a rejection of all forms of artifice.

Henry Bellery-Desfontaines, a decorative painter by trade and usually better known for his illustrations, reached a subtle balance in the table presented by Bellangé Company at the 1900 Universal Exhibition. His exuberant taste for sculpture was evident as was his preference for practical furniture, precluding ornamentation from the basic lines and table top.

As of 1897 the Sèvres National Manufactory joined the dissident camp led by the innovative ideas of its new art director, Alexandre Sandier. The conversion was spectacular. The program established for the 1900 Universal Exhibition excluded showing any forms or sculptures present at previous exhibitions.

Emile Gallé. *The Umbel Chair*. The model was created in 1902. Musée d'Orsay, Paris.

Emile Gallé. Study of cyclamen. Musée d'Orsay, Paris.

Following page:
Emile Gallé Cup *Roses de France*. In honor of Léon Simon, co-founder with Gallé of the Nancy Horticultural Society. Musée de l'Ecole de Nancy.

As proof of their sincerity, which was the most precious heritage that nature and plant study had passed on, the execution of the pieces had to be carried out at one go, without touch-ups or mounting. More than one hundred thirty new vase models were produced, in several different sizes. Most of these shapes were based on combinations of straight and oblique lines and the quarter circle, according to a systematic method set up by Sandier. By their volumetry, purity and manifestness, all of them harmonized with simple color backgrounds. A decor could also be added which corresponded to the form. It was the end of paintings reproduced on porcelain. It was equally the revival of almost exclusively floral ornamentation which took advantage of recent technical progress to create new color scales.

Table designed by Henri
Bellery-Desfontaines and
presented by the Bellangé
Company at the 1900
Universal Exhibtion. Musée
des Arts Décoratifs, Paris.

Studio of Emile Gallé. Vase design with metal mount. Musée de l'Ecole de Nancy.

Following pages: Manufacture Nationale de Sèvres. Group of vases with forms and decoration created between 1897 and 1908. Musée des Beaux-Arts, Nancy and Musée National de Céramique, Sèvres.

Maurice Pillard Verneuil.
Stained-glass design. *Etude de
la plante et ses applications aux
industries d'art*, Paris, 1908.

44

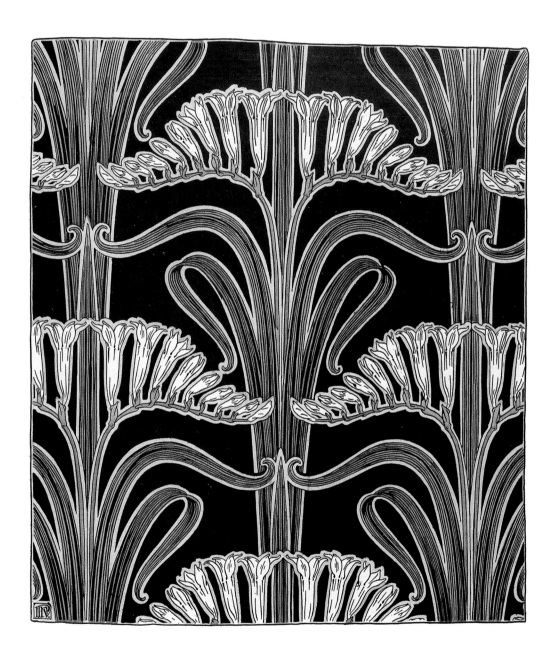

Maurice Pillard Verneuil.
Wallpaper design. *Etude de
la plante et ses applications
aux industries d'art*, Paris,
1908.

Lucien Lévy-Dhurmer.
Portrait of Georges
Rodenbach, 1896. Musée
d'Orsay, Paris.

WATER

In 1896 Lucien Lévy-Dhurmer exhibited a portait of the poet Georges Rodenbach, a pastel of impressive technical mastery, in the Georges Petit Gallery in Paris. Of Belgian Flemish origin, he settled in Paris definitively in 1887 during the height of the literary vogue of symbolism. His delicate silhouette stood out against the Gothic cityscape and the canals of Bruges: rather *Bruges the Dead* as he had called it in his novel in which he associated the city and its stagnant waters to his moods. In his collection of poems *Les Villes encloses* he returned to the same theme.

> "The waters of the ancient canals are feeble and mental,
> So bleak, amidst the dead cities, on the quays,
> Adorned with trees and rows of gables,
> Which are, on these sickly waters, barely traced…"

Emile Gallé. Glass hand with algae and rings. Streaked and marbled blown glass with applied decoration, 1904. Musée de l'Ecole de Nancy.

Léo Laporte-Blairsy.
Vase-Pieuvre (Octopus Vase).
Musée du Petit Palais, Paris.

Pierre Roche.
The Tadpole. Pewter teapot
presented at the 1895 Salon
National des Beaux-Arts.
Musée du Petit Palais, Paris.

These musings on water, which is so literarily evocative, carried with it a new
conception of the art object. The grammar of ornament, which was responsive
to an infinite variety of aspects in nature, was not usually attuned to the poetry
of elusive elements. For some time already, Gallé, like other glass and pottery
makers, had already placed the marsh dragonfly on his works. Inspiration from
Japan had already modified the design of aquatic fauna with a line of unexpected force. In an attempt to capture the fleeting impressions of ever-chang-
ing water, the strange inhabitants which seek shelter in it, and the mysteries it
encloses, decoration and form had to evolve concurrently and form could no
longer be dissociated from its covering. Hands dripping with algae, a terracotta
octopus vase, a pewter tadpole teapot graced the amateur's showcase of late
19th century sculpture curios.

Emile Gallé. *Red Algae.*
Small baluster vase with
algae and seashells. Cameo
glass. Private Collection.

Emile Gallé. *Starfish.* Round
bonbonnière with starfish.
Cameo glass.
Private Collection.

Next page:
Emile Gallé. Design for a
vase with algae presented at
the 1903 Exhibition of the
Ecole de Nancy at the
Pavillon de Marsan. The
conch form was created in
1884. Musée d'Orsay, Paris.

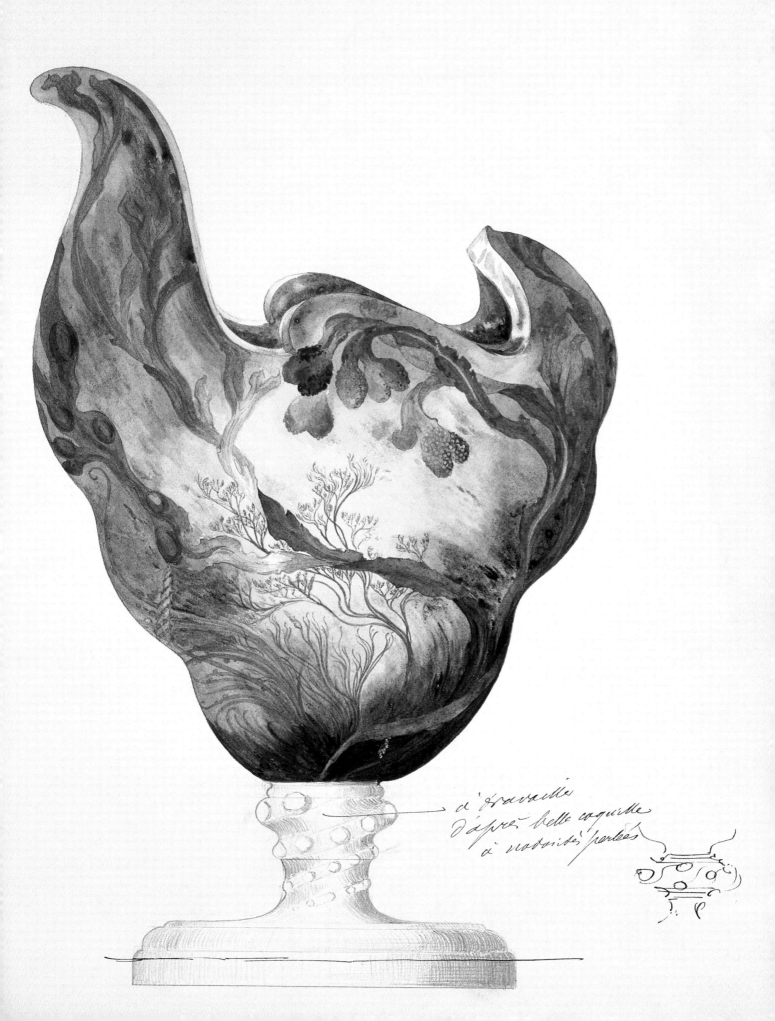

à travailler
d'après belle coquille
à nacrides perlées

Emile Gallé. Seashell. "Vide-poche Cup" presented at the 1894 Exposition des Arts Décoratifs de Nancy. The model was created in 1889. Musée de l'Ecole de Nancy.

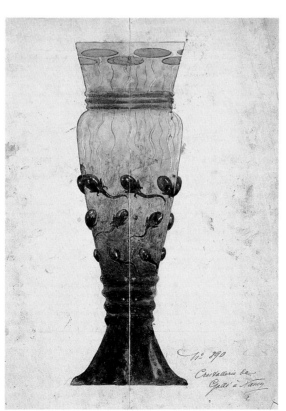

Emile Gallé. Design for *The Tadpoles* vase. n.d. (c. 1900?). Musée de l'Ecole de Nancy.

Emile Gallé. Water pitcher. (1904?). Musée de l'Ecole de Nancy.

THE CYCLE OF LIFE

Eugène Carrière. *Nativité*, 1903-1906. Musée du Petit Palais, Paris.

Jean Carries *Tête de bébé*. Sandstone. Musée d'Orsay, Paris.

Previous page:
Victor Prouvé. Drawing inspired by murals in the town hall of Issy-les-Moulineaux, c. 1898. Pastel and charcoal. Musée d'Orsay, Paris.

Could we confine Art Nouveau to the celebration of the plant world, without casting a glance at man and his moments of joy, passion and sadness? That was the task which the new decorative artists took on, to place man in front of his own image in vast compositions adorning the walls of public buildings and city halls. Without pedantry or excessive solemnity, while still abstaining from vulgarity, averting rhetoric and affected pathos, some abandoned historical references and refrained from exotic imitations. A parallel was drawn between the natural cycle and the important stages of life in a democratic republic. The artist was the commentator of a world in perpetual transformation, equitably administered by the laws of the republic.

Birth was one of the themes used to evoke the constant state of development. In one of his last works, *Nativité*, Eugène Carrière "the painter of the epic of human growth" wished to capture the anguish of that moment outside of time, when emotions are ambivalent, waiting for the infant to grasp his mother's breast and hence embark on his life.

Emile Friant.
Les Amoureux, 1888.
Musée des Beaux-Arts,
Nancy.

The kiss between a father and his son lends family life an unexpected and touching nobility of sentiment when Prouvé sketched the scene.

Emile Friant knew how to seize the quintessence in the most commonplace situations. It was his *Soir d'Automne* (*Les Amoureux*) that justly won him acclaim: its emotional impact is communicable. The scene was easily reconizable to natives of Nancy: on the Pont Cassé footbridge in the Grands Moulin district; a young couple, leaning on the rail of the metallic bridge, has stopped in a moment of amourous musing.

In *La Douleur*, a mother crushed by sorrow leans over the tomb where her child was just buried. Fearing that she might fall into the open grave, two relatives in deep mourning rush to restrain her. In the background, three women are weeping. One seems in despair and the second woman turns to console her. The third woman appears hypnotized by grief. In the far background, the men remain huddled together.

Emile Friant. *La Douleur*, 1898. Musée des Beaux-Arts, Nancy.

Friant's technique of photographic precision was inherited from naturalist painting of the 1880's. As for Eugène Carrière, he worked form, caressed and constructed it like a sculptor modeling clay without thickness. Shimmering with light and shadow, his blurred colors allowed realistic situations to take on depth and symbolic meaning.

The artist's symbolic language was composed of the elements most common to him, those which usually were considered anecdotal. With Carrière the most insignificant moments of life became events; in this he was a true artist of his time. He showed men what they never noticed.

His favorite theme was motherhood. The mother represented home life. She was its anchor. His family portraits showed the sharing taking place between the different members in a feeling of unity. There were also the portrait of the painter in all his different facets, at all the stages of childhood.

Chapiteau des baisers

André Michel. "La Sculpture décorative
aux salons", in *Art et
Décoration*, Paris, July-December 1899,
p. 35.

Emile Derré.
Chapiteau des baisers.

Folk art: it will not be academic art with its narrowness and its arrogant formulas reserved for a few initiates. It will not be romantic art with its earthy realism and often artificial literary lyricism. It will not be "realistic" art, if that is understood to mean an exclusive and sectarian doctrine which would mutilate life and reality and only extract from it ugliness and brutality.

Folk art is human art, and the folk artist is he who, when placed in an accessible nature, shows himself to be at times familiar and sublime, always unfailingly new; as long as man has eyes and hearts to contemplate and trust in it.

This is what Mr. Emile Derré wanted to say in his own manner in his sculpture, *Chapiteau des Baisers*. "Speak, my sweet images, carry tenderness and love to the heart!", he carved naively under the astragal. And on the basket where the rose, the vine, the olive and the ivy intertwine leaf and flower, he evokes the varied forms of human tenderness in the four groups. The impassioned kisses of lovers, the joyful kisses of a mother for her infant whom she devours with affectionate carresses, the sad and sublime kiss of forgiveness by a mother for her son now a man – that is to say, an ungrateful sinner whom life returns to her, battered and repentant, – and the farewell kiss of a son to his father... And as the artist, with a simple, sincere heart, bent down to draw deeply from the fountain-head of life and nature, he placed truth in his work.

Albert Bartholomé's Monument to the Dead in the Père-Lachaise Cemetery in Paris

Léon Bénédite. Excerpt from "Albert Bartholomé" in *Art et Décoration*, Paris July-December 1899, pp. 173-174.

Sculpture professors will probably be surprised by this work which departs from accustomed traditions to go back, one must say, to other traditions which are equally valid. No doubt, they will not find the usual vocabulary of their learned gestures, their authorized mimics and the accepted rhythm of academic canons. Obviously, neither the Greeks nor the Egyptians themselves, so dear to Bartholomé would have comprehended the painful theories of men in the violent explosion of such tumultuous sentiment. Their expressions were more measured, their eloquence more regular. They were certainly ignorant of all the lyricism and pathos which move us so deeply today. But in their narrow conception of human destiny, they had not felt the tragic breath from atop Mount Calvary which stirs us. Other times came, other already ancient times, which understood this and which we have since forgotten.

Certain penetrating minds then proclaimed a return to our ethnic traditions, Northern, christian traditions which draw the arts closer to our humanity. Despite the grand flourish of a very aristocratic art during the second half of our century, they had a presentiment of the crisis that sculpture would undergo, confined as it was in its eternal mythological dilettantism, in the narrowness of its anthropomorphic, pagan inspiration. Caught in a strange malaise, it faced, day after day, the inescapable problem of the expression of contemporary thought.

While Courajod, in his courses at the Ecole du Louvre, or Rodin, before his *Bourgeois de Calais* raised the banner of revolt against the obsession with pedagogical conventions, the Latin traditions established by the great 16th century Italian decorators, a few independant masters, preoccupied with making scupture speak a more lively, more moving language, tried to renew it by letting it express a democratic, social ideal, like Dalou or Constantin Meunier, or a more human, more impassioned, more expressive spirit, like Rodin.

Edward Steichen. Portrait of Albert Bartholomé, in *Camera Work*. Musée d'Orsay, Paris.

Albert Bartholomé, Monument to the Dead, Père-Lachaise Cemetery, Paris.

The tomb of Madame Jules Rais in Nancy

Clément Janin. Excerpt from "Un tombeau"
in *Revue des Arts Décoratifs*, Paris,
1902, pp. 97-98, 100.

The problem of death has always been present for humanity, who long sought a metaphysical solution and now inclines toward a positive solution. Many good minds, who were incapable of accepting this presumption of survival of the personality flattering to our pride, but which reality did not corroborate, have been won over by Auguste Comte's idea of "subjective immortality" through memory.

Ceasing to be theological, that is to say, general, this solution becomes sentimental, that is to say, individual. One believes what one wants and one wants what one loves. Memory enjoys the same freedom as affection; there are no limits. The most ordinary reaction to death is to purify it. In Sully-Prudhomme's poem *Bonheur*, Faustus tells Stella:

> I contemplate the beauteous heavens
> That darkness hid from me...
> What I dreamed about is here!
> All that I loved has remained there!

In this purification of death, everything base disappears from memory, and all that is venerated remains. Love on Earth having coming to an end, cult worship commences.

It is to this intimate and personal cult that the sculptural symbol which concerns us here is dedicated. Mr Pierre Roche executed it in collaboration with the architect Mr Girard, who oversaw its installation in the Préville Cemetery in Nancy.

Erected in this necropolis, surrounded by gravestones and crosses, the monument does not represent humble self-effacement, which would signify the resorption of the body in nature, nor vain-glory, which would mean incorporation in the divinity. It is both more dignified and more human. It is like the representation of the virtues, the qualities and the tastes of a woman swept away in her youth; her moral and corporal elegance, her natural goodness which were the attributes of this exceptional woman are materialized in its graceful curves. It does not speak of death, it recalls life. It expresses sorrow less than

it does the impossibility of forgetting and the ineffaceable mark of beauty on a mind who loved it.

It is a sentiment translated to endure in stone, bronze, ceramics and enamel. It is the sentiment of one man but becomes a general sentiment through its grandeur. In that, it differs from the funerary monuments produced during the great centuries of Art in Italy, France, the Netherlands and Germany. With the exception of the architectural arrangement, the elements could not be imitated, because each made exclusive reference to the person in whose memory the monument had been erected.

In substituting floral elements for the human likeness, Mr. Pierre Roche has created a classic. This monument can serve as a model, inspire similar ones.

Flowers have always been the tribute our piety offers to the dead, after having long been the symbol of their physical rebirth. Here however, the lily and the arum mean something else. They are the flowers from which a diadem was formed and placed on the deceased's brow: this diadem is visible on the pediment of the monument. The flowers represent her virtues and her inclinations. Intimately linked to her remembrance, they symbolize her qualities and recall her affections. In that respect, the monument is personal. But who can fail to see that this form of personalization in flowers is so slight that thousands can be characterized by them, in the same manner that the cross characterized their interior life?

It is precisely in this that the monument erected in the Nancy cemetery provides a new formula. While its point of departure originates in feelings for an individual, these feelings turn out to be so profoundly human, that the monument takes on the most general meaning possible. The lily and the arum could be replaced by whatever flowers one wishes. Henceforth, it will be known how to use flora as the dominant element of a monument instead of reducing it to the secondary role it has played heretofore.

But the fact that a concept is novel would be insufficient if it were not accompanied by the corresponding original form. This concept of a tomb does not express death as did Renaissance tombs which even went so far as to represent the deceased as a recumbent figure; to the contrary, it sees dying as the battle against death, the unjust Absolute, through the persistance of memory. A form was necessary to incarnat this exact concept, being both harmonious and solemn: solemn like the terrible reality against which our will is shattered; harmonious like life itself, which alone matters.

Several elements came together to interpret these feelings: firstly, the general lines of the monument, for this monument is above all line: secondly, the use of varied materials.

The whole monument is summed up by its crowning, in the lily which dominates. This lily does not have the limited signification which catholicism gives it in the hands of Saint Joseph. It remains the flower of tenderness and love in the *Song of Songs*. It also becomes the highest symbol of femininity which is proclamed in a prayerful impulse by the two words of the inscription *Purissimæ, pulcherrimæ*.

Everything leads up to this lily, and the monument itself is a sort of open vase where the whole plant is visible and from which the flower stem shoots forth into the air. And as the symbol is always included in the work of art, and even moreso in a work whose purpose is symbolic, the lower part of the lily, combined and enclosed in the structure of the monument, can be considered as the representation of our material life subjected to physical necessities, and the upsurge of the flower as the full blooming of our moral personality.

Mr. Girard, architect.
Funeral chapel for Madame
Jules Rais. Pré-1902. Musée
de l'Ecole de Nancy.

WOMAN

The paintings of Edgar Maxence (1871-1954) were largely inspired by English Pre-Raphaelism. The eeriness of his work can be largely attributed to the systematic use of the same process. The photographic precision employed for rendering the figures contrasts with the highly decorative background often reminiscent of a vaguely defined, undatable medieval style. Disoriented, the viewer is thrown into a world where the most innocuous detail takes on meaning. In *La Femme à l'orchidée* presently conserved at the Musée d'Orsay in Paris, the realistic treatment of the face and hands of the model stand out from the rest, where costume and plant ornamentation are one. The legendary princess dares to stare at us and, the height of anachronism, she is smoking. The resulting image is representative of the uneasiness pervading the late 19th century French republican society concerning the representation of women. For some time, and notably thanks to the revival of portrait painting within the naturalist movement in the 1880's, the representation of men was considered by genre fanciers as a worthy subject of psychological and moral study, whereas portraits of women were intended to capture a purely physical beauty and thus remained faithful to artistic conventions. In Maxence's 1900 portrait, although the figure was part of a setting which likens it to a decorative motif, the woman, pensive and active, was beginning to assert herself.

However, Georges de Feure still imagined her as a peacock; this is how he represented her on the walls of Bing's Art Nouveau pavilion at the 1900 Universal Exhibition when he imagined her as Joan of Arc, sometimes covered in armor from head to toe. For the graphic artist Alfonse Mucha, she appeared as a Byzantine empress, a fairy and a doll. For poster artist Georges Meunier she was a vulgar tart. The painter Jules Chéret imagined her as a Montmartre girl, mocking and arrogant. For the erstwhile rabelaisian Alexandre Charpentier, she adorned wine pitchers. This Art Nouveau was perhaps... new; but the new woman was yet to come...

Joseph Chéret. Vide-poches. Gilt bronze. Private Collection

Previous page:
Edgar Maxence. *La Femme à l'orchidée*, 1900. Musée d'Orsay, Paris.

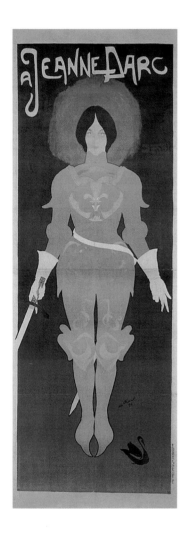

Georges de Feure. "*A Jeanne d'Arc*", 1896, Bibliothèque Forney, Paris.

Alphonse Mucha. Poster for Job cigarette papers, 1897, Bibliothèque Forney, Paris.

Jules Chéret. Poster for Job cigarette papers, 1897, Bibliothèque Forney, Paris.

Georges Meunier. Poster for Vichy mints, 1894, Bibliothèque Forney, Paris.

The case of Rupert Carabin remains an enigma. Detested by Henry Van de Velde, who perceived his work, and justly so, as the height of amorality and incongruity, Carabin nevertheless had his fans. Gallé in person congratulated him. Defender of unique pieces of furniture, Carabin regularly exhibited sculpture pieces in walnut like the "coffret à bibelots" presented at the Salon National des Beaux-Arts in 1897, which was acquired by the actor and collector of naturalistic works Coquelin Cadet. In it, Carabin grappled once again, with quite uncommon moderation, with his obsession for the savage woman depicted in a realistic manner. Despite a remarkable virtuosity with wood, his portrayal of nature and the primitive was so literal, with no apparent desire to intellectualize, that it was embarassing.

For the Art Nouveau jeweler, women however had not changed. The hair fashion for buns or chignons in the 1890's brought with it the need for hair pins and combs which, in the Japanese example, became true ornamental objects. The eroticism of women's hair was all the more emphasized. More restrained than René Lalique's jewelry, pieces by Lucien Gaillard attained a rare degree of expressiveness. No detail, no overworking detracted from the refined design and materials.

Previous page:
Rupert Carabin. Jewelry
case, 1897. Musée
de l'Ecole de Nancy.

Alexandre Charpentier. Wine
pitcher. Musée d'Orsay,
Paris.

Alfred Finot. *La Source* Vase,
c. 1900 for Mougin in
Nancy. Musée de l'Ecole de
Nancy.

Victor Prouvé. Feminine
figure in bronze on the *La
Parure* chest, 1894. Musée
de l'Ecole de Nancy.

Following page:
Louis Hestaux. Interior of
the *La Forêt* buffet, 1895.
Musée de l'Ecole de Nancy.

Models of the *Académie
d'arts décoratifs*. Layout by
Jehan Raymond.

Models of the *Académie d'arts décoratifs*. Layout by Jehan Raymond.

The Vallgren Soliflore Vase

Raymond Bouyer, "Quelques objets d'art des salons "in *Art et Décoration*, Paris, July-December 1898, pp. 22-24.

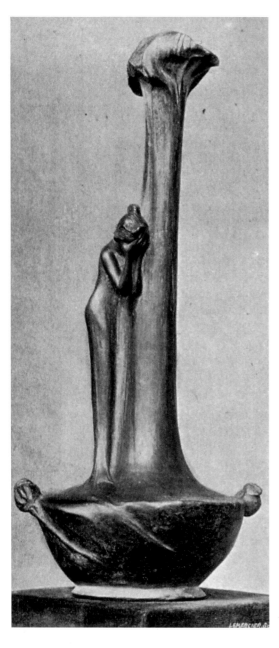

Vallgren is exquisite twice over, for he is a poet and he is simple. Let thanks be given for the candor of his art. In his chaste, somewhat timid work, this idea is not transitory, but immanent; the soul penetrates form and commands it, which is the case of a true artist. In his role as an artist, it is through the charming proportions, through a slender and profound realization that he sympathetically enters our very soul. The poem is born of supple matter. Gaze at the gracile Urn a long while. It is the best possible lesson in æsthetics. As for me, I never tire of returning towards its morose grace many a time. She has become my friend. I am in love with this half-woman, half-flower evocation, the siren of the plant world. And since art is exquisitely ignorant of jealousy, I want to share my conviction with others. To bring someone to love: is this not the greatest victory of human art?

"The points of view change at each instant" said Delacroix, and what is true for criticism, is even more so for sculpture, for the material, subtle statuary, isolated in space. This makes it possible to grasp the multiple aspects of a work which is mobile by pivoting its pedestal. How many times have I turned this melancholic Urn, this urn which is only ancient in name, but is, to the contrary, essentially modern. It is neither the harmonious *œnochoé*, nor the imposing lecythus, but one of the last incarnations of a mysterious dream, the last arrival from the interior city where thought inhabits, a funeral Tanagra where our Gérôme will not enter, and which underscores in poignant traits the divergency of the races. This is a delicate, plaintive series: a small, eloquent necropolis where adroitly draped, smiling courtisans no longer pass, nor the hired mourners whose gestures are admirable, nor the herculean victors of the arena, nor the whimsical histrions with their theatrical laughter: but an entire world appears, haunted by slender shadows embracing jealous urns, sobbing in the voice of the lines of the somber, hard matter mottled by a learned flame. And flowers spring up by handfuls... The Urn presents an adorable example.

How does such a poem blossom forth? Through what latent miracle does the familiar art object become a work with a soul? By the spontaneous mystery born plaintively of the indefinite lines, by the vaporous form wedded to the visible perfume of skillful patinas. The profile of virginal despair is delightful; two slender hands spoil the coquettish head of hair. The delicate sculpting of the young arms, the troubling nape, the emaciated back, bent in mourning, strangely sympathize with the stream-lined, juvenile, melodious curve of the bronze, of the crude, oxidized, rusted, verdigrised, marbled, charred, singed, rosy, reddened marvelous matter. The indefiniteness of a nude torso exhales from this plant, like from an opening flower. Several hesitations attest to the truth of the dream. Precise filigree line her fine hair. She weeps harmoniously, the frail Chloé from the North, and her anonymous, unknown, timeless sadness touches and arrests me like the affliction of a delicate passer-by. My memory binds me to this life sanctified by art. What melancholic rose will fade forever in this thin soliflore?

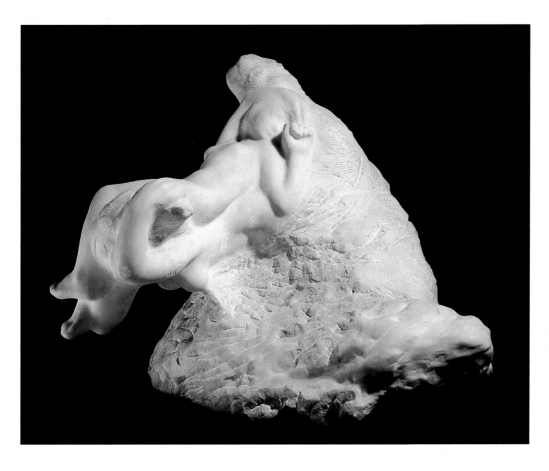

Auguste Rodin. *Psyché transportée par la Chimère.* Marble, c. 1907. Musée des Beaux-Arts de Nancy, on loan from the Musée Rodin.

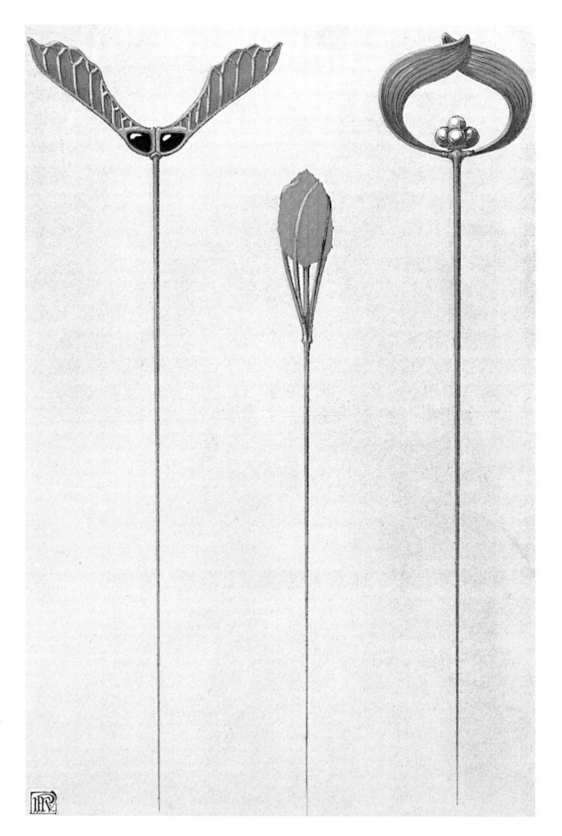

Maurice Pillard Verneuil.
Designs of hair pins, *L'Etude
de la plante et ses applications
aux industries d'art*, Paris,
1908.

Lucien Gaillard. Hair pin
Sycomore,1906. Musée des
Arts Décoratifs, Paris.

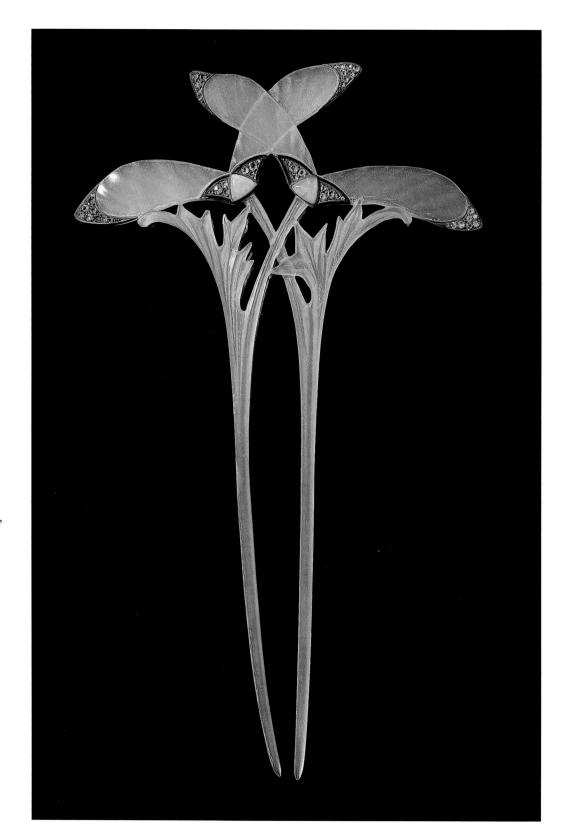

Georges Fouquet. Hair pin,
c. 1900. Musée du Petit
Palais, Paris.

Jules Desbois. Broach,
c. 1900. Musée du Petit
Palais, Paris.

Réné Lalique. Broach, 1898-
1900. Gulbenkian
Foundation, Lisbon.

DANCE

Art Nouveau and the performing arts converged thanks to an exceptional celebrity who inspired dozens of other perfomers during the 1890's. Adored equally by the most refined symbolists and the primitive naturalists, Loïe Fuller spent her childhood in Chicago. Her formative years as an actress, however, took place in New York and London.

Inaugurated in 1869, the *Folies Bergères* built its reputation on a repertoire very similar to that of an English music hall. Interludes with clowns, tightrope walkers and wild animal tamers shared the bill with vaudeville scenes. A large café set out as a winter garden attracted loose women and rakes, intriguers of both sexes, as well those who flocked here to laugh and flirt. A notorious haunt for prostitution, its atmosphere also provided inspiration for artists. In 1886 the *Folies* produced its first grand review. Three years later, electric lighting was installed in time for the 1889 World Fair. The Cream of Paris was drawn there.

Loïe Fuller's success seemed to indicate a refinement in audience taste. Her dance numbers associated ballet and pantomime. However, in the *Dance of the Serpentine* she frantically agitated waves of colored veils, thus creating a haunting luminous field around her. The illusion took form when the dancer came into sight. A stroboscopic effect decomposed her movements and an experimental use of artificial light projected onto the panels of her costume created original chromatic scales. In her different numbers – *Dance of the Butterfly, Dance of the Lily, Dance of the Lily of the Nile* (waterlily), *Dance of the Clouds* – she explored the synchronisation of movement and light which, as her act evolved, became matter for thought and sculpture. Her admirers regarded her performances as the materialisation of the union of Art and science, a flux of energy, and for Stephane Mallarmé "the dizziness of the soul, as if launched in

Raoul Larche. Sculpture with double lighting. Loïe Fuller in the *Dance of the Serpentine*, c. 1897. Private Collection.

Victor Prouvé. *Filles fleurs* (inspired by Loïe Fuller in the *Dance of Fire*). Bronze, Edition by Gruet, 1897; pâte de verre, edition by Daum, 1905; biscuit edition by Mougin, 1902. Musée de l'Ecole de Nancy.

the air by an artifice". Loïe Fuller embodied the esthetics of transformation, dynamic line and Art Nouveau.

At the Salon of 1897 the sculptor Agathon Léonard exhibited a series of plaster figures in a neo-Grecian style dedicated to music and dance; the poses are restrained and subdued. When the biscuit proofs of the statuettes were presented at the 1900 World Fair; entitled *Le Jeu de l'Echarpe*, they were very favorably received by the public. The hang of the dancers' and musicians' long-draped robes is reminiscent of Grasset's style. The movement of the long corolla-like sleeves, agitated by an invisible breeze, in the manner Loïe Fuller, proved that the representation of dance, even in its most classical form, had been marked indelibly by her hunger for life.

Manufacture Nationales de
Sèvres, Proofs of the
centerpiece,
Le Jeu de l'Echarpe inspired
by Agathon Léonard.
Presented at the 1900
Universal Exhibition in Paris.
Musée National de
Céramique, Sèvres.

WORK AS PERPETUAL TRAINING

Emile Gallé. *Les Métiers*
Buffet. Details of marquetry
panels, 1889. Musée de
l'Ecole de Nancy.

In the October 11, 1896, edition of *Le Journal*, Octave Mirbeau, in his regular column on contemporary art, imagined a monologue by the Italian renaissance painter Sandro Botticelli. It provided an opportunity for him to mount his combat against symbolism, against those "artists of the soul" that he rejected. "To produce a beautiful fresco, statue, poem or a pair of boots, natural talent is not sufficient. You must possess the knowledge of what you are doing. That is the theory, there is no other. It is knowledge which liberates us from the servility of imitations, which gives us personality… Knowledge is only acquired slowly through strenuous work… Life is perpetual learning and permanent emulation… I beheld life, nothing but life, and I saw around me, purity, faith, ectasy, joy, love, sin and sorrow, and nothing but designs… I avoided symbols, mystic rhebuses, intellectual intent like the plague, like ugliness…" Such was the profound opinion of Emile Gallé, who nonetheless recognized that within scientific experimentation there was a part of literary inspiration which gave free rein to symbolic interpretation; that distanced him from Eugène Grasset. Emile Gallé, the entrepreneur, had to elaborate a chain of decisions which were equally industrial and commercial in nature. While imputable to the powdery atmosphere of wandering clematis, astragena, ipomea, umbels and other lophosperms, the force of his dream celebrated life dedicated to study and the joy of work well done.

This was also the opinion of artists from the naturalist group such as Jules Dalou who echoed the opinion on this point of Neo-impressionist painters Paul

Signac, Maximilien Luce and Henri-Edmond Cross, as well as other Art Nouveau militants whose political positions are best left unmentioned. Socialistic after a fact, but not actually socialists: although they were undoutedly influenced by the writings of the anarchy movement, they shared a common love for work viewed as the source of all happiness. In Tolstoy, some found the exaltation of the primitive and sacred character of peasant labor. Others, upon reading Kropotkine, Bakounine or Elisée Reclus, placed work as a fundamental principle of the moral development of humanity. An amnestied communard who had actively militated for the creation of an art objects section in the Salon National des Beaux-Arts imagined a monument (never executed) to Work in 1897-1898. It was an erect penis, "Insignia of Priape, god of gardens, emblem of creation, roadmark of the cradle and tomb of the poor, of the chimney stack of the factory where his life took place".

For the 1900 Universal Exhibition Auguste Rodin created his *Tour du travail*. In this work, (which would remain at the model stage), a stairway guarded by two statues representing *Day* and *Night*, the sculptor attempted to embody Man's progression from the manual to the intellectual, and his drive for freedom. Paul Signac, whose pictoral research and friendships brought him close to Belgian Art Nouveau, exhibited his canvas *Démolisseur* in the 1900 Salon des Indépendants. The man at work became, according to Maurice Maeterlinck's expression, the "crusher of old hopes and defunct powers". In *Les Aubes*, a collection of verse which the poet dedicated to Signac, he had alluded to a future time, after the revolution had ended and peace was restored, when joyous gangs would wander singing through the city. Entitled *Panneau pour une Maison du Peuple*, the canvas was exhibited, and was to be accompagned by two others, *Haleur* and *Constructeur* to form a triptych as a tribute to labor and the awakening of the new society.

Emile Gallé. *Les Métiers*
Buffet. Details of marquetry
panels, 1889. Musée de
l'Ecole de Nancy.

Following page:
Eugène Grasset. *Le Travail,
par l'Industrie et le Commerce,
enrichit l'Humanité.* Project
for the Chambre de
Commerce de Paris, 1900.
Musée d'Orsay, Paris.

Aimé-Jules Dalou.
Le Botteleur, Le Rabatteur de faux and *Le Casseur de pierres*.
Musée d'Orsay, Paris.

Paul Signac. *Le Démolisseur*,
1897-1899. Musée des Beaux-
Arts, Nancy.

THE HOME

Following page:
Eugène Vallin. The Masson
Dining Room. Musée de
l'Ecole de Nancy.

Albert Besnard painted *L'Homme moderne* in 1887 for the School of Pharmacy in Paris; a replica of it is now conserved in the Beauvais museum. The figure is a meditative man with a long graying beard, who is reading on his balcony, overlooking the city. The book hangs from his hands, and deep in thought, he stares off into the twilight. Near him, the interior of an apartment and a lighted room where a child is doing his homework. A woman is setting the table near a lamp. Outside, the city below starts to light up as night approaches. A river, warehouses, docks with passing trains are visible. This small work can help us understand the world of Art Nouveau and especially the role that the home played in the laboratory of contemporary life.

The home was the place where the family unit came together, in a community where work, school and leisure were mingled. For the man who believed in a new art and a new society, the home was the nucleus around which amorous, filial and friendly kinship, intellectual and business relations evolved. These urbane, highly civilized customs mingled with impulses of generosity and confidence in a man living as closely as possible to what seemed to be his natural equilibrium and they necessitated outward signs of representation, even before they could function. Hence, complete suites of furnishings, from door latch to ashtray, started to show up in exhibitions, stores, houses of art or through exceptional private commissions. Everything had to be in the same homogenous style in order to be in phase with the thoughts of those for whom the objects had been made.

It was not an easy challenge. At that time, it was not considered to be in good taste to show one's desire to escape convention and especially to proclaim one's difference so abruptly in this manner. What's more, artists and furniture industrialists remained undecided as to exactly what image of modernity it was best to give, wavering between the conception of a new, more beautiful world that is is simpler and more rational and thus offers more justice and freedom, and a vision of the unusual and based essentially on the break between the past and the present.

The fireplace stood at the center of the modern interior. At Louis Majorelle's home in Nancy, it was housed in a large central pillar in the middle of the dining room, like the trunk of a giant hybrid plant species, finishing in two stools

90

Victor Prouvé. The Masson
Dining Room. Painted,
hammer-wrought leather
repoussé panels, 1905.
Musée de l'Ecole de Nancy.

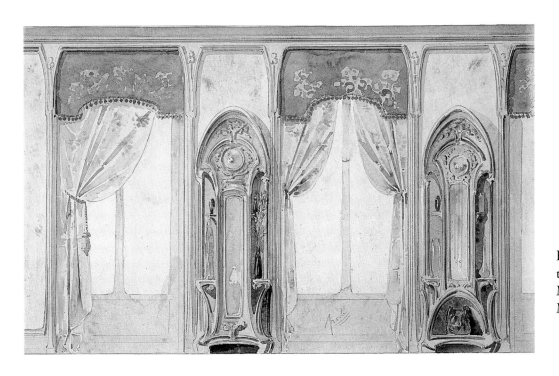

Eugène Vallin. Project for the Masson dining room, rue Mazagran, Nancy, c. 1903. Musée de l'Ecole de Nancy.

Eugène Vallin. Project for the Villa Bergeret dining room, Nancy, c. 1903. Musée de l'Ecole de Nancy.

Henri Sauvage and
Alexandre Bigot.
Fireplace, *Villa Majorelle*,
Nancy, 1902.

Alexandre Charpentier. Dining room designed for Adrien Bénard's home, Champrosay, 1901. Musée d'Orsay.

providing seating on each side of the fire. It had been modeled first in plaster under the watchful eye of the architect Henri Sauvage before being fired piece by piece in ceramist Alexandre Bigot's kilns. Around the fireplace, and often directly attached to it, a network of wood panelling branched out along the walls. Within this architecural framework, buffets and sideboards were installed, sometimes even a parquet clock or a large thermometer-barometer as in Charles Masson's dining room. In Adrien Bénard's home in Champrosay in the Paris suburbs, a fontaine was included, executed by Bigot and by the sculptor cum decorator Alexandre Charpentier.

Although most of these commissions of exceptional breadth concerned dining rooms (occasionally bedrooms or the master library), smaller works throughout the house were an opportunity for the movement to express itself in the home context. The stairway in large town houses often was decorated with ornamental ironwork and stained glass. Stained glass was often present in the conservatories in high favor in the 1880's.

Louis Majorelle. *Orchid
table*, c. 1906. Military
Command, Nancy.

Louis Majorelle. Meuble de
salon with Seaweed motifs,
c. 1904-1905. Musée de
l'Ecole de Nancy.

Following page:
Louis Majorelle. Staircase
handrail, Bank Renauld,
Nancy, 1910.

Jacques Gruber. Stained glass
window with peacocks and
doves, c. 1904. Musée de
l'Ecole de Nancy.

Previous page:
Louis Majorelle. Handrail
of grand staircase, *Villa
Bergeret*, Nancy, 1904.

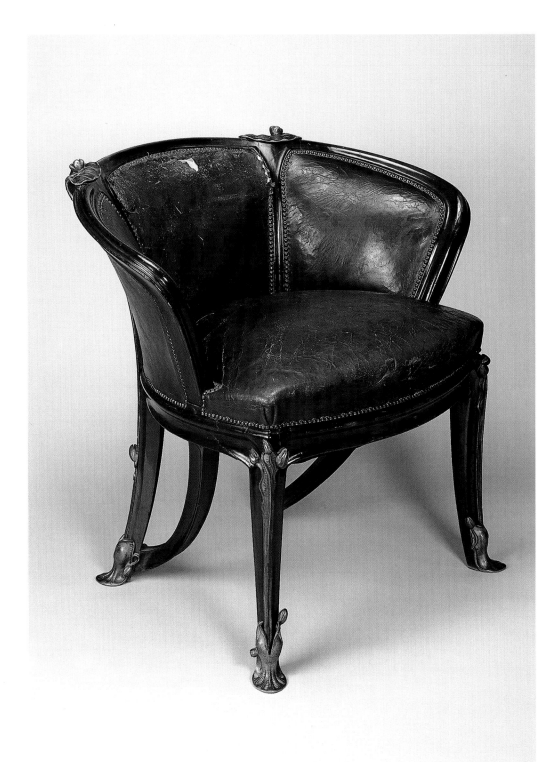

Louis Majorelle. *Waterlily*
Armchair, 1900.
Musée de l'Ecole de Nancy.

Louis Majorelle. *Waterlily* Table, 1900. Musée de l'Ecole de Nancy.

Louis Majorelle "the father, par excellence, of French modern furniture in the rich, ornate style"

O. Gerdeil, "Les meubles de Majorelle" in *L'Art Décoratif*, Paris, October 1901, pp. 24-25.

Louis Majorelle. Floor clock and armoire presented at the 1901 Salon des Artistes Français.

Where the faults of the School of Nancy come home to Mr. Majorelle, and stand out as a blemish on an otherwise excellent production in many respects, is in the compositions executed in marquetry, covering the panels of a whole category of pieces. The introduction of a landscape, a flower still life or a scene with animals is incompatible with the decorative effects to be distributed throughout the apartment where the piece will be placed. This has already been mentioned; there is no use belaboring the point. As regards the use of marquetry, it seems infantile when used in this type of scene. When something can be done with a brush and several tubes of paint, you must really have time to lose if you try to achieve the same effect by a technique a hundred times more complicated. Good marquetry is beautiful work, of course, but wanting it to be a substitute for painting, means it is no longer art, but rather falls into the category of puzzles.

Besides, the compositions which serve as pretexts to this marquetry work are defective from a decorative standpoint. Instead of being synthetic and producing rhythmic lines, they are diffuse, confused, lacking mordacity. In a word, they are, I am sorry to say, the art of Nancy at its most tiresome.

How superior Mr Majorelle can be when marquetry is not employed in his furniture and the flat surfaces owe their interest to the wood itself! In this category – and the desks illustrated belong to it – it is difficult to surpass Mr Majorelle. Exploiting fully the freedom of treatments, he has the tact never to go beyond the point where fantasy of forms becomes eccentricity. He knows how to dose sculpture for a piece so that it is rich and representative without overdoing it. He possesses that rare gift of being fashionable while remaining simple. His variety is endless. He is the father, par excellence, of French modern furniture in the rich, ornate style.

The bronze mounts which Mr Majorelle has been using for the last two or three years on this type of furniture have been well accepted. My personal feeling leads me to prefer no metal in furniture outside of the locksmithing, but I can easily recognize the attractiveness and good taste of Mr Majorelle's applications of metal. Their placement, design, patinas: everything combines to make them elegant, attractive ornamentation.

With its qualities and its faults, furniture produced by Mr Majorelle is and will continue to be in vogue, because it suits our inclinations perfectly. It is not desirable that they inspire a school of followers, because it takes all the talent of their creator to ensure that their good points – which are his good points – override the bad ones – which are those of where he was born and lives. Their value, in fact, goes beyond, that of a passing fashion. The pieces which survive will one day be collected and cited as characteristic of one of the phases of the irresolute times we are experiencing.

Furnishings for a yacht

Joseph Balmont. Excerpt from "Lucien Magne et son enseignement", in *Revue des Arts Décoratifs*, Paris, 1901, vol. II, pp. 405-406.

We shall give special notice to the decoration of the yacht *Hélène*, constructed for the distinguished amateur, Mr P. Mirabaud. Mr. Lucien Magne demonstrated on this occasion the adaptability of his talent, which combines judgment, rigorous observation, and science as much as imagination. He was faced with totally new and very modern problems, because in a ship the decoration of each room must fit in with the structures of the construction and meet specific conditions. Art and science must be in especially perfect harmony on a yacht. The architect had to combine furniture, seating, tables, electric lighting and totally original forms. The dining room table, for example, posed an interesting problem because of the camber of the boat. The fifth leg in the middle of the table had to be equipped with a counterweight system, and the other four with eccentrics to be able to regulate the height, taking into account the slope. To this end, the legs were fitted out with adjustable copper cases. Mr. Magne was able to overcome these difficulties and transform them into decorative ressources.

Lucien Magne. Deck house dining room on Mr. Mirabaud's yacht, *Hélène.*

Daum and Majorelle. *Prickly pear* lamp, c. 1902. Musée de l'Ecole de Nancy.

OBJETS D'ART

The history of Daum glassworks in Nancy at the turn of the century is synonymous with the success of the alliance of art and industry. "Mr. Gallé is an inventor, Mr Daum is an excellent continuer who is beginning to invent" could be read in *La Lorraine-Artiste* in 1896. The following year the Daum company continued to command interest as it participated in the Universal Exhibition in Brussels. At the Universal Exhibition in Paris in 1900, it obtained the Grand Prize in the glassware category. Nineteen lamps were presented by Daum that year. Suddenly, the wealthy clientele could abandon the heavy faience and metal models for more stream-lined, graceful ones where the transparency of glass allowed light to play on the changing tints of the engraved decoration. Ushering in the lighting revolution and associating this still uncommon new source of energy with traditional know-how, Daum showed its genius. At the beginning, the glassworks prudently continued production of oil lamps, introducing amusing effects that played on infinite refractions. The two distinct parts of oil lamps, the belly and the globe, allowed for a variety of decorations. On the belly, forest undergrowth and mosses would grow. To add to the charm of the scene, several glass snails would chase each other. On the upper half, a simplified decoration of flowers and insects (flitting butterflies or dazzled, fluttering maybugs on the light source) surrounded the globe, filtering the soft light. For electric lamps, the forms could be even more original, freed as they were from the oil reservoir and the wick key. Orchid, waterlily, prickly pear, and dandelion lamps were outfitted with bronze mounts by Majorelle; this turned out to be a very opportune commercial alliance between the two companies. Later, the bronze splints were replaced by a glass structure; a bulb was placed in the lamp body which was completely separated from the light under the shade.

Parallel to the success of its lights, Daum diligently developped a line of vases which were sharply in demand. Gallé had been the first to develop glass without ever thinking of presenting the technical side of fabrication, even doing all that was possible for it to remain invisible. Daum, to the contrary, showed off its expertise. Plant ornamentation should reveal the fact that it has been blown, molded, multi-layered, acid-etched, wheel-carved, hammer-wrought and sometimes then completed with applications.

Daum and Majorelle. *Dandelion flower* lamp, c. 1902. Musée de l'Ecole de Nancy.

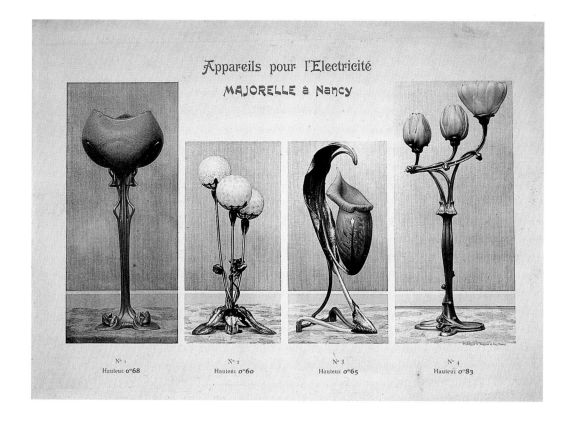

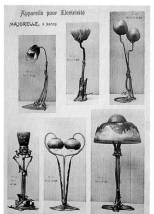

Pages from the *Catalogue des Etablissements Daum*, c. 1902. Musée de l'Ecole de Nancy.

Glasswork was not the sole applied art to enter modern interiors. Silverwork would also profit from the infatuation with Art Nouveau. In *Documents Décoratifs* published in 1902, Alphonse Mucha presented designs of several silverware patterns. Jules Habert-Dys imagined a quite strange, zoomorphic soliflore vase As for porcelain, with the collection of small Sèvres vases with crystallizations, it seemed to detach itself from the exclusive use at the dinner table. Here Far Eastern influences encountered the arabesques of the bronze or silver mounts. This precious world of egotistical contemplation shut off from rational study cohabited in the house with another world which was orientated toward playful or intellectual activities, without the two ever meeting. While Alexander Charpentier was designing a lectern or a closet for storing the instruments of a string quartet, or door plates decorated with musical or game motifs, the artists from Nancy were concentrating their efforts on pyrogravure and leather marquetry for the bindings of their dearly loved books.

Daum and Majorelle.
Waterlily lamp, c. 1903.
Musée de l'Ecole de Nancy.

Alphonse Mucha. Plate from
Documents décoratifs, 1902.
Musée du Louvre, Paris.

Electric candlesticks edited by Goldscheider and
Ulmann

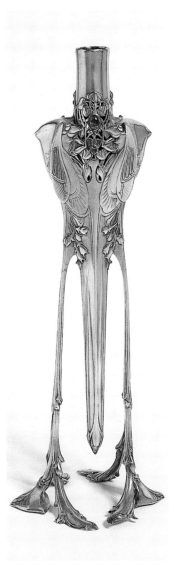

Jules Habert-Dys. Porte-
bouquet, 1906. Musée
du Petit Palais, Paris.

Manufacture Nationale de
Sèvres. Left: Neuilly A vases.
The form was created in
1897.
Decoration and mount were
created in 1904.
Right: Marne vase.
The form was created in
1903. Decoration and
mount were created in 1904.
Musée national de
céramique, Sèvres.

Manufacture nationale de
Sèvres. Chevilly vase. The
form and the decoration
were created in 1898.
Pair of Igny A vases. The
form and the decoration
were created in 1897. Musée
National de Céramique,
Sèvres.

Daum. *Horse Chestnut in Autumn* Vase. Detail, c. 1908. Musée des Beaux-Arts, Nancy.

Following page:
Daum. Left and center: Vases with blackberries, 1910; right: Vase with wild roses, 1910. Musée des Beaux-Arts, Nancy.

Pages 113-114: Daum. A grouping of vases with floral decorations, 1898-1904. Musée des Beaux-Arts, Nancy.

Daum. Cup with maybug. Detail, c. 1905. Musée des Beaux-Arts, Nancy.

Preceding page: Vase with bouquets of daisies. Detail, c. 1897. Musée des Beaux-Arts, Nancy.

Clock, c. 1902.
Private Collection.

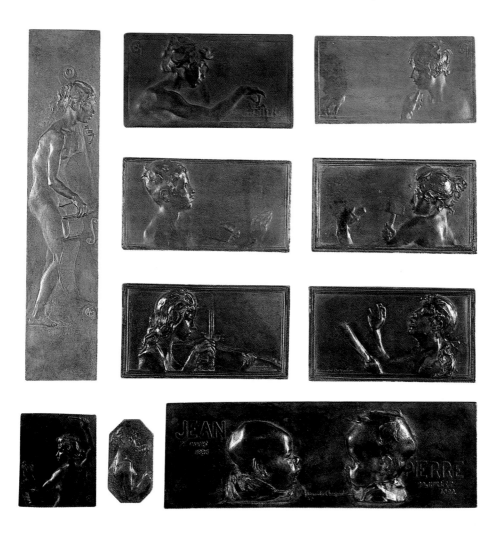

Alexandre Charpentier. Door and key plates. The models were created between 1893 and 1897. Musée d'Orsay, Paris.

Camille Martin.
Bookbinding, *L'Estampe
originale*, 1894. Musée de
l'Ecole de Nancy.

Jehan Raymond. Writing
pads with incised calfskin
covers. Models from the
Académie d'arts décoratifs.

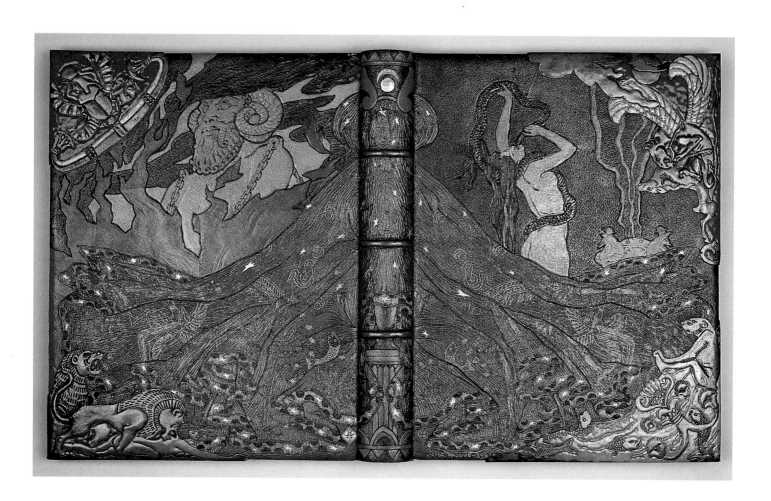

Victor Prouvé. Bookbinding. *Salammbô*, 1893. Musée de l'Ecole de Nancy.

The professional training of art craftsmen

Emile Gallé. Excerpt from "Mobilier
contemporain orné d'après la nature"
in *La Lorraine*, Nancy, January 1, 1900.

Do you know that men of my generation, despite all the progress accomplished, found themselves very hampered when they began their career. We were creating decorative art, producing even very skillful furniture in France, and the journals *Le Monde illustré* and *Le Magasin pittoresque* have left us images of them. They show that we were scarcely capable of doing anything but repeat old themes.

Some, it must be said, who were absolutely enamored with the Renaissance, forgot to be modern, or even to be French. Italy worked its seductive charm on them! Some spent all their time in the Cluny Museum. There was classical furniture, as there had been before, but more justifiably so I think, a Clunisian architecture.

How, then were the young men prepared, who were destined for the decorative fields? I must confess that, in my case, during my training I did not receive all the elements that were necessary to facilitate the beginning of my career. No professional training was given to art craftsmen, with the exception of recruits who handled drawing pens and easels. Before 1789 to the contrary, trade guilds very logically dispensed training simultaneously in techniques and in the corresponding decorative applications. In other areas, the guilds were tyrannical. They were abolished and rightly so. But what was an error was to disassociate the two areas of training. Fabrication skills were dispensed in Conservatories while resources and virtuosity – drawing, painting, modeling, composition – were taught in Institutes. Nowhere were theory and practice for each and every artistic craft ever brought together through tutorials and pratical exercises. In short, no master to teach methods and process, to adapt flora and fauna to suit various techniques and materials. No one to apply artistic means for the different trades which depend on nuance, line and artistic inventiveness. No archiving professional instruction. No overview. No traditional continuation. Quite a few false ideas and an ignorance of the state of decrepitude bordering on barbarism. Such was, around 1863, the professional initiation of young people destined for decorative fields when they left secondary, professional, painting or architecture schools. The artistic craftsman was treated like a dog thrown into the river to teach it how to swim.

True, there was actually *fake drawings* as, after the establishment of archeological museum, there later were *trades which produced imitations*. What could someone do who lacked the nececessary flexibility to spend his whole life reproducing works from the past?

Fortunately, and I must again speak for myself, the love of flowers reigned supreme in my family, a hereditary passion. It was my salvation. I had some inkling of natural sciences. I was well acquainted with Godron's botanizing, the author of *Flores de Lorraine et de France*. My father reproduced drawings of grasses and flowering pastures of crystal and porcelain. Following in the paternal tradition, I developed form and decoration on glass and clay. I proceeded by trial and error, with groping and fumbling that special training could have spared me. In the end I had to do the same for furniture, experimenting with the same application of principles, the same adjustments of decoration which I had drawn from life.

And when I produced some examples of contemporary furniture decoration, the first lesson I learned was that it is advisable in decorative art, as well as in the other arts, to understand Beauty as Truth and never in the erroneous and mediocre sense of prettiness without character or opulence stripped of spirit. The most practical advice which can be given to decorators seeking figurative elements for furniture is that they find them in organic life and treat them in a truthful manner.

"An art full of natural well-being, lively, human and true"

Emile Gallé. Excerpt from "Mobilier contemporain orné d'après la nature" in *La Lorraine*, Nancy, January 1, 1900.

At the convergence of creative forces, posterity will not find anarchy in contemporary furniture or in the other decorative arts but rather, in the same vital spirit, furniture with generous modern characteristics presented as the traits of a happy family: personality, individuality, reflexion, concern for logic, observation of nature, emotion, imagination, enthusiasm, sincerity and life.

The decoration of modern furniture will have expression, because the artist, in contact with nature; cannot remain indifferent to the nobility of organic forms. There are no sincere sentiments which are not communicable to others. Touched, the artist of modern decoration will become capable of touching others, of leading other men to share his emotion. These works will please, charm and move sometimes by their beauty; the decoration will be eloquent and fraternel. The decoration of modern furniture will show no bias of melancholy. It will be sincere. It will therefore be willingly joyful, because it will be an art of the masses, that is an art in which the worker, the executant, instead of being reduced to the state of a machine and only knowing the "hard labour" of producing parts of works by others, by the sweat of his brow, without being able to embrace the finished piece, will be raised to the dignity of consciousness. He will also be called to take his part in just remuneration for intelligent work and the free joys of the spirit: knowledge, conception, invention, interpretation of a plan, of a work and the adaptation of organic models to the handcraft. This art can thus be joyous, because it will be interpreted with pleasure, with consciousness by the worker. The executant ornamenter will be freed from servile copy, dulled by things devoid of meaning, reality and charm.

In summary, contemporary furniture must be logical, comfortable, artistic, full of natural well-being, lively, human and true or it will be nothing. It will not exist for art, we feel, no more than does many a product catalogued among the various styles.

Emile Gallé. Dining room furniture. Salon National des Beaux-Arts, Paris, 1903.

Emile Gallé. Dining room furniture. Salon National des Beaux-Arts, Paris, 1903.

An office-study for a busy man

Franz Jourdain. Excerpt from "Tony Selmersheim" in *Art et Décoration*, Paris, July-December 1904, pp. 195-198.

This ever so discreet grouping includes all the characteristics of modernity and resolves the complicated problems of present day existence with utmost intelligence. The always restricted space at our disposal, whatever the situation or fortune may be, on the one hand, and on the other hand, the multiple needs brought on by a civilization which is more and more anxious, more refined, and more desirous of well-being places the decorator before almost insurmountable difficulties. Mr Tony Selmersheim did not waste an inch of space in the room which is a salon, an office and an art gallery all in one.

All latitude is left to the owner's imagination and choice, freeing him from bothersome symmetry or obligatory fittings; the smallest corners are utilized and each element of the grouping enhances the display of cherished curios.

The upper board becomes a running shelf where bronze, pewter and ceramic pieces, and also statuettes are displayed without pedantry, a temptation to the eyes and hands. The corner sofa has been advantageously rounded off to provide comfortable seating for conversation. The wall decoration, which is only interrupted up to head level, continues to render expected, valuable services. The fireplace is not only a source of heat for a period of several months but also a showcase. And, in fact, the library with its shelves, drawers and wardrobes is three pieces of furniture in one.

Make no mistake, this desire to condense everything, to combine everything, to organize everything provides an admirable answer to unformulated, but tyrannical needs. The overheated life we lead demands a sordid organization of time. To waste a minute or an hour appears an aberration or a calamity. Opening a door, crossing a room, looking for a book, rummaging through a box perched on top of a tall piece of furniture is frightening and boring. A busy man will be infinitely grateful to the artist who can anticipate needs which he has not even imagined, who can bring within reach the most frequently consulted books, everyday papers, key documents and also several personal art objects which add a little joy to the everyday work and battle.

Tony Selmersheim's furniture was designed in the vein which I have just briefly mentioned. If I had the time to develop the subject, I would add that this way of understanding interior decoration and furnishings relates to ideas of the highest moral standards. It is not only interesting for the wealthy and middle classes, it englobes the working and the lowly classes, whose tastes have been emprisoned in lies, shoddy goods, fake sumptuousness, imitations and ridiculous copies of inaccessible luxury. A Louis XV mirror wardrobe in a working class household shows shocking, almost painful stupidity. Bought necessarily at an absurdly low price, this wardrobe with its horrid, roughly-carved pediment will fall apart in several months and will be out of place in modest surroundings. The wife of this honest worker has no need for a full-length mirror for her personal hygiene. It would befairer, more logical and honest to sell him a solid piece of furniture in light-colored oak with harmonious proportions in which the manufacturer has placed a shelf for several books next to the household linens and another for a warmly-colored ceramic pot by Bigot.

We hope that Tony Selmersheim will continue his courageous undertaking. May he deliver us from the horrors invading us. Through his talent, may he also generalize simple, pragmatic, inexpensive furniture. He can then be justifiably proud of having gotten rid of the most absurd and dangerous of systems that France has ever known.

Tony Selmersheim. Office-study, *Art et Décoration*, Paris, July-December 1904.

Georges de Feure's Studio

O. Gerdeil Excerpt from *L'Art décoratif*, Paris, January 1902.

If it is true that a home is the reflexion of the person who lives there, the images of Georges de Feure's studio reproduced on these pages must somewhat baffle the readers who contemplate them. I can easily imagine that the painter of those fantastic creatures, women of incredible litheness half transformed into snakes and sphinxes, hiding the enigma of disturbing traits under the immense waving feathers of a hat which none of the milliners in the Notre Dame de Lorette district would dare create is fancied as a sort of Barbey d'Aurevilly, someone possessed who surrounds himself with accessories, among which a book bound in woman's skin would be the least bizarre.

We must put things in proportion. The now famous artist whose nomination to the Légion d'Honneur was celebrated by a banquet for eighty of his friends is infinitely less black than that.

It is true that he was part of the group of young painters for whom the late Léon Deschamps became the impresario and of which the fairly macabre trials graced the small salons of *La Plume* eight or nine years ago. At that time, a strange epidemic spread through the studios of the young, from Montmartre to Montparnasse, an affection which doctors supposedly would have called "gynophobia" if they had had to treat any cases. None, unfortunately, were submitted to their attention. Distrust of women, a feeling aroused by the first experiences with the fair sex and the manifestations of which go no further for normally constituted men, changed into terror for the young artists stricken with the illness. Women appeared to their haunted minds as horrifying monsters, and their hallucinations overflowed onto small terrifying canvases where the woman-peahen soared over heaps of cadavers, skulls, femurs and tibias against a background of flames or boulders hurling into the abyss. In the foreground, grovel flocks of men transformed into toads, swine and other lowly creatures.

Was Mr de Feure part of that generation? Did he go through that crisis? Despite several small canvases which were slightly wild and a certain series of *Femmes damnées* inspired by Baudelaire, I think he only bordered on it. Actually, his theories concerning the "eternal woman" were only a pretext for purely decorative images, his incomparably delicate tones enhancing their strange quaintness. That he shows this in a slightly upsetting light is a question of pure dilettantism. For these variations he chose what he thought to be an amusing theme, and one which indeed is.

Be that as it may, as a painter, Mr de Feure is one of to those from whom the disconcerting is expected in all he undertakes, and those who only know his canvases may be surprised to see him in such a discreet interior. It is far removed from the interiors of others who, through the pretext of modernism, take pleasure in innumerable pecularities in the form of furniture and interior architecture. To honor his role as apostle of the revival of decorative arts – and one of the most brillant apostles – the master of the house did not deem it necessary to look for difficulties where there are none, as they say. Nothing is less likely to shock the viewer than these pieces of furniture; like all good furniture, constructed of panels fitting into rectangular frames, and of seats where nothing is to be remarked precisely because they are solid and comfortable. If it were not for a few details, very discreetly distributed, where the artist's potent imagination has left its mark, one could almost consider the furniture as quite ordinary. I believe it is healthy to say – for one should not miss an opportunity to combat the idea held by some many people concerning modernism in the applied arts field – that what is modern must be something which over-throws all the existing habits. No belief retards progress more than this, for it causes the public to dislike all innovation while only promoting the most extravagant. We should show opposition to this bothersome prejudice through the example given by innovaters for whom the madness for newness at all cost does not cloud their talent. Among them, is Georges de Feure, one of the most bold.

Georges de Feure's Studio.
L'Art décoratif, Paris,
January 1902.

Furniture as seen by Serrurier-Bovy

Roger de Felice. Excerpt from
"Le sentiment architectural dans
l'ameublement", in L'Art Décoratif,
Paris, November 1904, p. 198-200.

We have chosen a certain number of M.G. Serrurier's latest furniture creations because they are, so to speak, architect's furniture in its purest state. The construction of each piece was guided by rigorous logic; each is the development of a thesis, a new idea. As in a geometry theorem, everything is linked. We could almost say they are schematic. These last years, our readers have been able to follow the evolution which led M. Serrurier to the rational outcome of his guiding principles. Not too long ago, the "movement" of his pieces turned to gesticulation, and the use of metal sometimes appeared indiscreet. Nothing of the kind now subsists.

Nothing has been surrended to decorative fantasy. There is not a single detail which does not have its utility, which cannot be explained by technical necessity. Everything has a function, a practicality. Every table, every sideboard, every showcase should be closely examined to appreciate the sum total of technical research their realization represents, while seeming, at first sight, so straightforward. Take for example this small woman's desk, to which two screen panels have been added, one on either side. This fusion of two pieces of furniture into one is not a caprice, it is the answer to specific needs. The two mobile panels give the desk added stability as well as filling out its silhouette, which otherwise would be too gaunt. Its height would also seem disproportionate to its width, but in fact, added width is not useful. When they are brought forward, the panels protect the person from drafts and indiscreet glances; they add a feeling of self-communion and tranquility. On raising and lowering the desk flap, we were quite surprised by its extraordinary lightness. This comes from the counterweights hidden in its structure which defy gravity, making it easy to handle for even the most fragile female hand. To obtain the necessary steadiness, the hinges of the flap must be very solid. For this purpose, they have been reinforced with polished copper strap hinges covered with smart decorative motifs. Angles have been reinforced with corner irons which also add to the sober, refined richness of the desk.

The tea table-showcase, almost completely made of crystal plates is a very delicate, slender piece, but one in which everything comes together to ensure maximim stability. The large solid base defies bumping; all angles have been rounded off to avoid snagging passersby. To prevent the tediousness caused by excessive rectilinearity, the curved bottom of the frame of each crystal partition forms a small ledge. Could this be a purely decorative detail? Not at all, for these shelves become shelves when folded down and the ledges rest against the back of the showcase and maintain the partitions horizontal. A corresponding analysis can be carried out for each piece of furniture.

By the pleasing disposition of its varied elements, inscribed in a pure, simple whole, and by the correct distribution of weight on the successive planes on which light can play, the dining room sideboard shown in the illustration also seems to comply with a distinctive architectural spirit. The same is true for various bench-showcases and bench-bookcases – favorite themes for Mr. Serrurier – which are so difficult to carry off successfully in such a way that the asymmetry does not destroy the unit.

The shortcoming of such a purely rationalistic conception of furniture is a certain stiffness and poorness of appearance. M. Serrurier does not avoid this all the time, but he is a colorist extraordinaire. A potent, audacious colorist and this quality makes up for all and, most of the time, gives his furniture a true sumptuousness. It is he who comes to mind when we mention the most successful color harmonies used in decoration. No one handles it with greater mastery and the reproduced watercolor can only give a pale idea of what is truly a feast for the eyes. Sometimes the harmonies are soft and subtle, more often audaciously vibrant – red orange padouk, bright yellow polished brass, deep blue fabric – these symphonies are never gaudy. It is common knowledge that Mr Serrurier allows no one to finish the decor accompanying his furniture. He himself designs and directs the execution of wallpaper, floor and table rugs, draperies, gas, electric and petrol lamps; fireplaces, stoves and all types of decorative ironwork. In this manner he succeeds in creating decorative ensembles of high standards and of such rare unity that the unequaled equivalent is not produced by France industrial manufacturers.

A complete suite furniture for 1,200 Francs

Frantz Jourdain. Excerpt from "Le Mobilier au Salon National des Beaux-Arts" in *L'Art Décoratif*, Paris, 1903, pp. 212-213.

As regards social needs, Mr Bénouville has very intelligently understood them by concentrating his efforts (finally!) on small budgets. I have been advising artists for such a long time – *vox clamans in deserto* – not to concentrate only on millionaires and to work also for the lowly. This is, I must confess, the realization of one of my heart's fondest dreams.

For the relatively reasonable sum of 1,200 francs, Mr Bénouville has produced a solid, well constructed, complete suite of oak furniture with a charming appearance: bed, wardrobe, buffet, tables, chairs and shelves. Nothing is missing and everything has an artistic, rational, gay, honest, delightfully correct air. How far we are from the falsehood, shabbiness, from infamous rough sculpting, peeling veneer, warping doors, curling inlaid moldings! All that ugly, pretentious and uncomfortable furniture that is sold at shamelessly high prices to workers, perverting their taste, must disappear. The furniture of a rich bourgeois has nothing in common with that of a worker, who has no need for outward signs of representation. A housewife, who also does the chores of a cook, chambermaid and servant and must take care of her husband and three or four children, has very little time to dust Louis XV scrolls and Henri II balusters. And such Louis XV! And such Henri II!

An interior thus decorated with harmony and good humor is the enemy of the bar, it is the doctor of that filthy affliction called alcoholism. When a man is happy in his own home, he will forsake the way to the sordid drinking holes and will appreciate the comforts of family life.

On the rough fireplace in his room M. Bénouville placed two blue and gray ceramic pitchers filled with bunches of wallflowers. Oh! What a happy thought! Violets, daisies, poppies, cowslips, this simple bouquet is the ideal decoration, and one within everyone's means.

Léon Bénouville. Dining room. Salon National des Beaux-Arts, 1903.

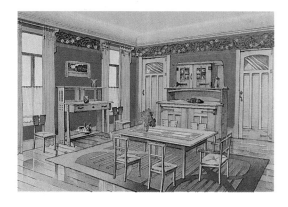

Gustave Serrurier-Bovy. Dining room. in *L'Art Décoratif*, Paris, November 1904.

MODERN HOUSES AND APARTMENT BUILDINGS

Louis Bonnier. Design of a Paris boulevard with two-level traffic, n.d. Institut Français d'Architecture, Paris.

In 1896 the Prefect of the department of the Seine formed a commission on which most members were architects; their task was to prepare a code for public thoroughfairs. The architect inspector of the City of Paris, Louis Bonnier, designated as recording chairman, had just completed the layout for the Salon de l'Art Nouveau gallery for art merchant Samuel Bing. Here his task was to illustrate the report with drawings which would show the profession the changes introduced by the project from the double viewpoint of technique and esthetics. The new code allowed for projections on a third of all façades giving on the street. On sufficiently wide streets ornamental additions and tiered levels could be decorated much more exuberantly than before. The decree signed in 1902 brought new life to architecural creation. The façade competition which the City of Paris had organized since 1899 offered substantial advantages to prize-winning real estate owners and encouraged contractors to take part in stimulating emulation.

Louis Bonnier. 1902 public thoroughfare code. Perspective of the upper part of a building more than 20 metres high. Institut Français d'Architecture, Paris.

Paul Charbonnier.
Apartment building, 3 rue
de l'Abbé-Gridel, Nancy,
1902.

Lucien Weissenbürger.
1, boulevard Charles V,
Nancy, 1904.

Lesser known than Guimard, but also considered as an avant-gardist, the architect Charles Plumet created a model, which in more or less adapted forms was successful in Paris and in the provinces. Meticulous care was given to the bonding of the slightly shaped façades and their ribless relief work, but the real interest was higher up, in the long stone gallery and the excessively elongated gable windows. Charles Plumet, Georges Chédanne, Louis Sorel, Louis Bénouville, Paul Auscher and later Louis Charles Boileau and Auguste Herscher were also to find Paris an interesting proving ground, although their styles were less provocative than Guimard's.

Nancy was possibly the least populated of the Art Nouveau centers but wasn't lagging behind. Between 1902 and almost 1909, the date of the International Exhibition of the Eastern France, several very characteristic buildings of the movement were constructed. Villa Majorelle (1902), rue du Vieil Aître, by Henri Sauvage; the Huot House (1903), quai Claude Le Lorrain, by Emile André; the Victor Luc House (1904), rue de Malzéville, by Jacques Hermant; and Villa Bergeret (1904), rue Lionnois, by Lucien Weissenbürger: those four examples alone bear witness to their homo-

Huot House, 92-92 bis quai
Claude Le Lorrain. Emile
André architect, 1903.

133

Jules Lavirotte. Award-winning façade, 29, avenue Rapp, Paris, 1901.

Jules Lavirotte. Building boulevard Lefebvre, Paris. *La Construction moderne*, June 23, 1906.

geneity and singular drive. It was proof that the Paris-Nancy axis (Sauvage and Hermant lived in Paris) was capable of highly satisfactory results. Elsewhere in the city, work on form and tradition borrowed from the medieval vocabulary was visible on dozens of buildings (for example, the elongated pinnacle decorated with plant forms surmounting the gable window on one of Weissenbürger's houses). Sculpted effects were omnipresent and intimately connected to the architectural conception of sculpture (the central bay and the curve of the balcony of one of Paul Charbonnier's houses). There was also the pleasure of combining fine materials in order to have light play off them (superposition of millstones, local stone from Euville, traditional and glazed brick and faience tiles).

In fact, during their continued experimentation and efforts to carry them out to a more or less satisfactory conclusion, the elaboration of a model of modern accommodation faced two types of difficulties. Firstly, to progress, architecture requires a firm commitment from those producing it in favor of the present and the links with tradition they wish to protect or eradicate. Secondly, for those who had already made up their mind, the solution resided in the pursuit of a type of communal habitat, for the greatest number, embracing the moral values which the utopia of "Art everywhere and for all" espoused.

The luxurious apartment building at 29 avenue Rapp in the 7th district of Paris, built by architect Jules Lavirotte, one of the prize winners of the 1901 façade competition, rather resembled a Neo-Rococo fantasy. (The stoneware covering gave it the necessary trappings of modernity in the public's eye.) Five years later, the same architect completed a building of low-rent public housing on Boulevard Lefebvre with a totally different appearance. Decorative wood-work and half-timbering, porch roof covered with glazed tiles enlivened the façade which on this occasion, was inspired by traditional construction. Whether this was due to the architect's sincerity or changing fashion, is diffi-cult to say. Organized by the Rothschild Fondation in 1905, this competition concerned welfare housing in the capital and the penchant of the organizers for the picturesque style was common knowledge. Formerly expressed in by plant and organic motifs, the call of the primitive and an asserted attachment to the earth, led some to regionalism. Two years after completion of Villa Majorelle in Nancy, Henri Sauvage and his associate Charles Sarazin finished an austere-looking building on the rue de Trétaigne, in the Montmartre area of Paris. Appearances were misleading. In an attempt to counter companies prompted by philanthropic intentions but also interested in investing their capital under excellent conditions, the Low-Rent Hygenic Housing Company Limited sought to establish a manifesto. In an economic context completely different from the one they had known when they were commissioned by wealthy patrons, Art Nouveau architects found the direct interpretation of what they were seeking. Being unable to break with the bourgeois conventions of hous-ing, they invented new ones, more beautiful ones according to them, for the masses. The care taken in the public areas was particularly remarkable. The building as foyer took on meaning. The ground floor housed a working-class university, complete with library and conference rooms, a food cooperative, and a healthy restaurant. In the center of the building, a large stairwell opened up, with a distinctive cast iron and copper guard-rail meticulously designed by Sauvage. All the floors, even in the apartments, were poured cement which could be waxed like a parquet. No paper on the walls, just enamel paint. All around the walls of the room, moldings had been mounted so that the occu-pants could hang pictures without damaging the paint. On the roof... a hang-ing garden.

Henri Sauvage. Low-rent building, 7 rue de Trétaigne, 18th district, Paris. Street façade. Institut Français d'Architecture, Paris.

Louis Bonnier. Villa
La Bégude, Cagnes-sur-Mer,
1900. View of the façade.
Institut Français
d'Architecture, Paris.

But the times had changed; no more complacent militantism. For the person of independent means simply seeking a little fresh air, Louis Bonnier designed a prototype of the well-constructed, non-nostalgic country home. Here the preoccupations of the defender of new values joined his interest in country life. Photographs of *La Bégude*, built in 1900 in the hills of Cagnes-sur-Mer, by the Parisian architect of Samuel Bing's Salon de l'Art Nouveau, leave the viewer perplexed. From the exterior, it was a traditional Provencal farmhouse; from the interior, there was a fireplace and benches in the style of the English architect Voysey. It was Art Nouveau with simplified forms, practical and lively, where rare wood marquetry lost out to a plaid tablecloth.

Louis Bonnier. Villa
La Bégude, Cagnes-sur-Mer,
1900. View of the dining
room and a bedroom.
Institut Français
d'Architecture, Paris

137

Henri Sauvage and the Villa Majorelle in Nancy

Frantz Jourdain. Excerpt from *L'Art Décoratif*, Paris, August 1902, pp. 204-205, 208.

The architect carefully, or rather instinctively, avoided the grave error of dressing up a commonplace idea in original trappings. It is not only the exterior which frees itself from the pedant yoke of the Institute, it is the whole, the vision, the general spirit of the composition which expresses youth and vitality, invention and ingenuity.

First giving his attention to the subject at hand, Mr Henri Sauvage endowed the Nancy villa with a special character, that of a dwelling which is neither vain nor sumptuous, that of a dwelling which is neither the residence of a parvenu nor of a prince, that of a dwelling which does not seek to attract the envy of passers-by through a show of false ostentation. We imagine it to be the home of a sensitive, busy artist, with a cultivated mind and a delicate eye, worried little by the judgment of others. His only desire is to live a clean life in a lofty, intelligent and pure atmosphere.

The architect's first concern was the plan, and he took loving care in the pratical appointments, with little concern for stupidly sacrificing the conveniences of the inopportune existence of the elevations. The main façade faces north, but only the rooms of secondary importance, those which are simply used on certain occasions, like the staircase, receive northern light. This is also true for the studio. On the other hand, the bedrooms receive southern light. In the same manner that the room have intended purposes, the four façades are all different, not from a craving for the bizarre, but as the mathematical solution to a given problem. This absence of symmetry not only permits the plan to be read like an open book, without trickery, but the entire construction takes on a delectable fantasy. Thanks to the

architect's candor, the eye follows the ascending staircase, enters the studio through the vast glass roof, makes out the privacy of the bedrooms, stops near the small windows of washrooms, pauses in the spacious, hospitable dining room; and inspects the vestibule. It is a slightly rustic vestibule, one which doesn't pastiche an urban antechamber, an agreable vestibule that can stand muddy feet coming in from the garden, one where the air smells of flowers and trees.

In juxtaposing the façades on the plans, leaving the first tributary to the second, the architect renews, in fact, the sacred tradition of the Greek style and the Gothic style, the tradition of the true classical style which can tolerate no trickery, or falsehood. This respect of the truth he applies with as much rigor in his decoration, which proves to be impeccably rational, conceived at the same time and in the same movement as the house construction, like the consequences of an idea, the corollary of a theorem.

He studied the orientation of each room, as I have already mentioned above, respecting intended purposes and needs which are frequently contradictory and cancel each other out. He then turned his attention to proportioning the windows to the cube of the space of the rooms to be lit, assigning to the windows the best possible place for light diffusion. He calculated air circulation and the heating necessary for each room. Using the solutions of these different problems, constituting the main features of his *scenario*, he then patiently reduced the form and the location of the windows which play an almost indispensable role in the elevations. These numerous, unfamiliar concerns, I must confess, will probably cause a surprised or disdainful smile to appear on the lips of many virtuosi who, in

architecture, are only worried by the majestic ordering of a façade and the symmetric alignment of windows like a company of Prussian grenadiers throwing light either on the feet, the belly or the head of the occupants. They create windows which indifferently open onto an insufficient washroom or an oversized salon, windows which are cut off by a staircase, or by the floor of an ill-conceived garret; mute, stupid windows which ignore what goes on behind them and appear to be in the midst of a recitation for junior collegians. These concerns, however, form the basis of the most honest and the sincerest of the arts, to which we owe the masterpieces in marble, granite and stone, the pride of humanity.

Let M. Henri Sauvage continue down the path on which he is treadding! Works like the Villa Majorelle will teach us more about 20th century architecture than the Opera Comique of the palaces, great and small, on Alexander II Avenue.

Henri Sauvage.
Villa Majorelle, Nancy,
L'Art Décoratif, Paris,
August 1902.

Charles Plumet and the modern home

Excerpt from the brochure signed by the Group of Six,
quoted by Pascal Fortuny, "Charles Plumet" in *Revue des
Arts décoratifs*, Paris, 1899, vol. I, p. 150.

"It is from both an artistic and asocial concept that we intend to interpret plastically, an expression chosen voluntarily for its simplicity, within the grasp of everyone. Through the representation of a display of pure reason, we hope to impress minds by utilizing the means with which the materials of modern construction provide us to the service of the most humanitarian and democratic ideas."

"[…] To tell the truth, we are proud to believe that the artist, by essence enamored with humanity, is on a fundamentally altruistic mission: to put before the eyes of man, even in the most humble things of life, the greatest amount of reason and never compose anything for daily use which is not based on utility united with beauty."

"The day is not far off when every man of upright character and clear vision will come quite naturally to admiring a beautiful civic action and the beautiful line of a domestic object using the same deductive powers and analytical reflexion."

"[…] We are singularly invigorated in our faith in the idea guiding us by our immense love for truth, by our hate for all those who wish to impose the colonnades, arcades and attics of an art foreign to our race as modern style, and finally, by the daily spectacle of the bastardized art which the street offers us."

"Our purpose is too lofty from a sociological point of view, our moral interest too great to complete the proposed work, for us not to realize already, and joyfully so, that we must make available to this purpose, with apostolic self-sacrifice, all that is burning within us of creative passion, an unshakable will to succeed and unselfish abnegation."

"We shall be rewarded beyond all expectations in soon witnessing the profound evolution which will be the consequence of the reform is modern housing."

"Man, henceforth, will take possession of the new decoration executed for him and the principles of sound logic, rationalism, will once again grow in the good earth of France. Having once again become a better man, he will recognize the ancient, direct and, no matter what is said, imperishable qualities of his race."

Left and previous page:
Charles Plumet and Tony
Selmersheim. A working
class house. Interior and
exterior views. 1903 Home
Show, Paris.

Eugène Vallin. Projects for the Gaudchaux and Delchard display windows, Nancy, 1901. Musée de l'Ecole de Nancy.

SHOPS AND RESTAURANTS

Above all, a shop front should attract attention and present the merchandise on sale in the best possible manner. Should all efforts be made to make it absolutely different from what had been conventionally accepted up to then?

The contribution of the carpenter, cabinet-maker and sculptor Eugène Vallin was instrumental in some of the most noteworthy realizations in Nancy. The best example, judged by the importance of the project, was the show windows of François Vaxelaire and Company on rue Raugraff. The architect Emile André collaborated on the project which was completed in the early months of 1902. The two lower levels of the building on the street were entirely gutted. A wooden framework was installed in front of the metallic structure. The large mirrors of the ground floor were connected to those of the second floor (behind which were the new dressing rooms) by a network of ribbing reminiscent of plant forms in the outline of the moldings and the way in which they were assembled. At the entrance, a geometrically-patterned iron gate designed by André in the style of the ironwork adorning the nearby Gaudchaux and Delchard store marked its direct filiation with the architecture of Paul Hankar from Brussels.

Contests for façades, contests for signs, contests for mailboxes were supposed to perpetuate the first efforts undertaken to make streets picturesque, with the support of the art and architecture journals and the Union Centrale des Arts Décoratifs. The slogan "Art in everything", which played its role in the success of Art Nouveau by firing the curiosity of the general public, also had its reverse side. Based on copies or whimsical imitations, products of mediocre quality had

RESTAURANT BOUDET. — PROJET D'UNE PARTIE DE LA FAÇADE.

Léon Rudnicki. Restaurant Boudet, at Boulevard Raspail and rue Léopold Robert, Paris, c. 1903.

Louis Majorelle. The bar at the brasserie *Julien*, rue du Faubourg Saint-Denis, Paris.

sprung up almost spontaneously. Their curious ties with fashion endangered the credibility and survival of the movement. People around the turn of the century ran on steam and electricity and not on pencil drawings by a designer of arabesques. The modern beauty of the wide shopping avenues, for example rue du Quatre Septembre and rue Réaumur in Paris, owed little to formal, insipid details of a precious, pretentious art. Throngs of people filed by, street-cars passed by the hundreds, joyful jumbles of things were everywhere, dozens of large gold-lettered signs decorated each story of the buildings. Wasn't it enough to animate the ground floors of shopping streets? They had to be entic-ing, rational, easy to clean and maintain.

Participating in the street spectacle, but intended as places of leisure as well as of consumption beer halls and restaurants in the Art Nouveau style multiplied. On Rue Royale in the capital, not far from the silversmith Christofle and the upholsterer Jansen, the painter Léon Sonnier and the architect Louis Marnez decorated the restaurant *Maxim's* with light mahogany panelling in early 1899. Reflected in the numerous mirrors, the yellow copper fittings shined against the pastel tones of the mounted canvases. At the same time, Hurtré and Wielhorski

Hurtré and Wielhorski.
Design for the restaurant
La Fermette Marbeuf,
rue Marbeuf, Paris. *Art et
Décoration*, January-June,
1899.

Henri Senet. Main dining
room of the *Restaurant des
Fleurs*, 277, rue Saint-
Honoré, Paris, 1903-1904.

installed the restaurant *La Fermette Marbeuf* in a courtyard under a metallic-
framed greenhouse. The walls were filled in with ceramic panels decorated with
aquatic plants, flamingos and peacocks. The carpet design represented mysterious waters teeming with frogs and horseflies.

The ultra-chic *Restaurant des Fleurs* (1903) by architect Henri Senet, located
at 277 rue Saint-Honoré, transposed the new style to the Court of Louis XV
with a debauchery of ornamentation. Attracting a more working class public,
the *Taverne de Paris* at 2 avenue de Clichy was closer to the Montmartre atmosphere. Above the sofas, gilt bronze electric bracket lamps on the curved wood
panelling covered with fans, were reflected endlessly in the mirrors. In the first
dining room three painters (Willette, Grün and Steinlen) evoked Gay Paree and
the atmosphere of the district. Jules Chéret decorated the staircase landings
while Abel Faivre and Léandre took command upstairs.

Jules Hermant. Decorative
panels for the restaurant
Taverne de Paris, 2, avenue
de Clichy, Paris.
La Décoration moderne,
1905-1906.

Bruno Möhring, with *La Maison Moderne.* Restaurant *Konss,* rue de Grammont, Paris. *L'Art Décoratif,* Paris, 1900-1901.

148

A German Restaurant in Paris

Do you recall the German restaurant of the Exposition? Perhaps not. Everything goes by so quickly in Paris and the Exposition already seems so far away! Iron skeletons of what were its monuments are still standing and of the enchantment of the white city, all that remains is a fuzzy picture in our minds, seen through the mists of oblivion.

The German restaurant was in great vogue, the place at the Exhibition. People had adopted it. It was good form to meet there in large parties. Tables were reserved one or two days in advance. People arrived late, dined and drew out the evening as long as possible so that they had to face the promenades of Paris only once the throngs had left.

Building on fleeting fashion became the point of departure for a lasting entreprise. The director of the German restaurant at the Exhibition, Mr Konss, the owner of one of great hotels of Berlin and a very skillful man in his field, repeated in the heart of Paris what had worked so well for him on the Quai d'Orsay, now called *Cosmopolis*. It was a daring plan but in business, there is no success without audacity.

At the Exposition restaurant, however excellent the cuisine and wines may have been, the real attraction was the rooms. Berlin architect Bruno Möhring created a curious place, an example of the new German art which France had not yet seen at all and which was presented under the exceptionally favorable conditions of a village fair to which everyone who came was determined to have a good time. Mr Möhring's talent brilliantly adapted to the circumstances. Unrefined, not delicate, it was to the contrary robust and carved out by a hefty arm with heavy axe strokes. It was exactly what was necessary for a place destined to exist for a short time, then perish. The restaurant on Quai d'Orsay was an exhibition attraction in the best sense of the word and its success was completely deserved.

Were Mr Möhring's strong points also put to good use on the Rue de Grammont, where his task was not to welcome exhibition visitors but rather guests navigating daily in fashionable circles and opulent surroundings, far from the daring of this new art? It is a question which is for a French author difficult to answer.

The character of the establishment is the purely German and nothing is more difficult than to judge things which are not of your own country. We are caught between two obstacles: spontaneous exaltation and incomprehension. Therefore I shall voice my opinion for what it is worth; it is my opinion, nothing more.

Mr Möhring's modernity seems unreliable to me. It is obvious that the artist has given new forms to everything, that he wanted to produce effects which have not yet been encountered through the use of countless combinations of materials, or unusual treatments of materials. He gave original character to each decoration. I do not see the connection between the impression that the whole inspires in us, between the state of mind that the surroundings cause in us, and the spirit of the times. A wind of heroic barbary passes over this rude, violent and incoherent magnificence and we do not know how to come in contact with it. The people we hear in this place are not thoughtful, methodical, eloquent Germans, speechifying even at the table, *de omnire scibili*, of meticulous politeness and dignified formalness – and even less so Parisians. These are heroes from fabulous epochs. Instead of frockcoats and hats from Madame Desfontaines, it is the shiny scales of coats of mail that the tables call for. I think I hear the rattling of bronze rings and the clashing of shields set down noisily by new arrivals against the robust feet of the divans.

In considering, as do many of his compatriots and a certain number of our own, the strange and the unusual as being synonymous with modernity, Mr Möhring was mistaken. To be modern, it does not suffice to do something different from what everyone else does. One must create surroundings in relation, not so much with the material resources of our times (that happens naturally), but with our state of mind and the bent of our spirit. They are characterized by a scientific trend of thought through which reason commands, ever more imperiously our impressions of everything extraneous to passion, through a vision of beauty which refines itself by simplification…

G. M. Jacques in *L'Art Décoratif*, Paris, November 1901, pp. 54-56.

Bruno Möhring, with *La Maison Moderne*. Restaurant *Konss*, rue de Grammont, Paris. *L'Art Décoratif*, Paris, 1900-1901.

THE UNIVERSAL EXPOSITION

The Universal Exposition of 1900 was in planning from 1892. A law concerning it was voted in 1896 and despite the critics – provincials, and among them the Nancy contingency, complained of its gigantic proportions, saw it as the triumph of centralization and questioned its commercial opportuneness – the supporters won out. Between April 14 and October 27, 1900, the event welcomed 51 million visitors.

The 112 hectares site was spread out on both banks of the Seine. Line 1 of the Paris subway opened on July 19, followed by the Alexander III Bridge, the Grand Palais, the Petit Palais, Gare d'Orsay and the Invalides train stations... It was not a time for introspective meditation. Never had a similar event included so many attractions. The choice was vast. A tour around the world under the Eiffel Tower? Enter the Maréorama for a several minute voyage between Villefranche on the French Riviera and Constantinople? A ride on the Transiberian train (with stops at the main stations between Moscow and Beijing)?

And what if we took the Modern Style circuit?

We shall leave to others the patriotic and laborious job of throwing flowers at the heterogenous heap of largely temporary buildings in broken brick, mortar and carton-pierre which composed the major part of the Exposition. The Institute enjoyed crowning moments in the official palaces but an active, audacious enemy was there to torment the victor.

We begin our tour at the monumental gate on the Place de la Concorde at the bottom of the Champs-Elysées. Three arches formed a triangle. Its outer covering of thousands of gaudy red and blue cabochons recessed into staff actually hid electric lightbulbs. It was like walking under a huge sea creature; the design was by the architect René Binet, a great admirer of Ernst Haeckel and his

research on micro-organisms. A fascinating curiosity. Rue des Nations was a
masterpiece. The Finnish pavilion was situated there. No overstatement. A sober,
robust building. The young twenty-five year old architect, Saarinen, had imagined a homogenous entity to express the soul of his country through an evocation of primitive beliefs, warrior legends and ancestral poetry. In the Palace of
Industry the most remarked stands were those presenting musical instruments
designed by Jules Hermant, leather products by Léon Bénouville, paper products
by Lucien Sorel, the Costume Jewelry stand arranged by André Arvidson; the
Fine Jewelry stand which surrounded that of Tapestry by Charles Risler.

Near the Seine stood a monster of iron, the Schneider Pavilion, named after
a cannon merchant and lord of the city of Creusot. After painting it red, Louis
Bonnier had transformed this artillery turret into a death machine at rest. The
progressists could not help but notice the German delegation, with its Hunting
Room by Bruno Paul, Study by Bernhardt Pankok and Drawing Room by the
Darmstadt artists colony. On the Esplanade des Invalides near Alexander III
Bridge, stood the Grand Guignol designed by the architect Henri Sauvage in
the "Art in the Street" section. The Union Centrale des Arts Décoratifs pavil-
ion was built onto the Invalides train station, next to the "Printemps" and "Bon

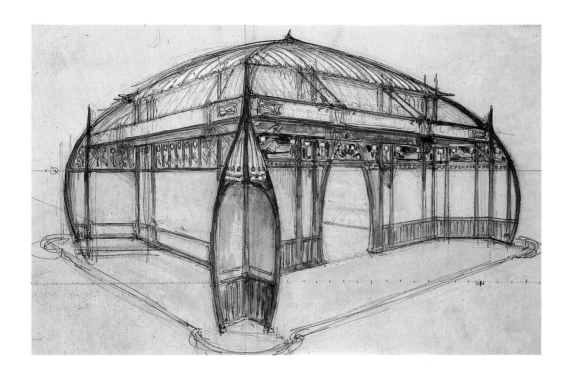

Marché" department stores pavilions. Fitted out by the wealthy decorator and collector, Georges Hoentschel, largely with his own money, it had a cabinet d'amateur or "Salon du bois" at its center (reassembled in the Musée des Arts Décoratifs in Paris in 1905). In the four corners, showcases presented artists'products from the previous decade. A large decorative canvas by Albert Besnard, *L'Ile heureuse*, hung on one of the large panels.

Further along, on rue de Paris, stood the Loïe Fuller Theatre, also designed by Sauvage. The plaster walls seemed to tremble as if covered with drapery. Charles Plumet who designed the interior decoration constructed stalls separated by great mahogany masts standing in enamelled ceramic bases from Alexandre Bigot's kilns. Two astounding sights not far from the Eiffel Tower: the Clément and Guérineau ceramics pavilion designed by Henri Provensal and the smart *Restaurant Bleu* by Gustave Serrurier-Bory from Liège, who was associated with the Parisian, René Dulong. Their boutique in the capital, *L'Art dans l'Habitation*, 54, rue de Tocqueville, opened in 1899. Here our walk comes to an end.

Now let's talk about projects, architecture on paper. Architecture which now only exists in archives. For example, the "Art Nouveau Bing" pavilion, in the garden of the foreign delegations on the Esplanade des Invalides. The one

Louis Bonnier. *Globe Elysées-Reclus*, 1900 Universal Exhibition, Paris. Institut Français d'Architecture, Paris.

hastily constructed that we haven't mentioned yet attracted little attention. Designed by André Arfvidson and decorated with exterior panels by Georges de Feure, it replaced another possibly larger project imagined by Louis Bonnier. The same Louis Bonnier designed an incredibly ugly kiosk, but also, and more worthy of our attention, a terrestial globe, which was to be erected on the Trocadéro site. Conceived as the Eiffel Tower of the 1900 Exposition, this 60-metre tall pavilion had been designed with the collaboration of geographer Elisée Reclus. It was a globe to the scale of 1cm = 5 km. Its only purpose was pedagogical and of course its monumental size. Inside the sphere, on the ground and first floors, a reception area, documentation and exhibition halls were to have been constructed.

Georges Hoentschel. *Salon du bois* presented at the 1900 Universal Exhibition, installed in the Musée des Arts Décoratifs in 1905, Paris.

Art Nouveau and the Modern Style in question

Victor Champier, Excerpt from "Une salle à manger" in *Art et Décoration*, Paris, 1901, vol. II, pp. 337-343.

It would seem that when speaking of "Art Nouveau" or of "Modern Style", one is using expressions which are sufficiently clear that they should not lead to confusion. Well, that appears to be an error. Taken one after the other in contradictory senses, these expressions are sowing the seeds of discord. They are giving substance to the most heated discussions and incredible misunderstandings since everyone is interpreting them in the most arbitrary fashion and wielding them as M. Prudhomme did his sword, he who was ready to defend the Constitution or if need be, combat it. Depending on the occasion, the partisans of Art Nouveau are considered sometimes as enemies, sometimes as champions of Progress. In fashionable even bourgeois circles, where occasional questions of art are willingly discussed, it is a sport much in vogue to ask the guests after dinner:

"Ah, what do you think of the Modern Style?"

The answers crisscross, followed by empassioned and confused comments in the midst of which certain artists'names explode like bombs: Gallé, Lalique, Grasset or traditional clichés: "The genius of France"; "What use is a new style since we already have so many ancients olds which the world envies"; "Taste is the prerogative of aristocracies"; "People have the furniture they deserve." "In art, there is evolution, not revolution…" I could go on and on.

Generally these discussions admittedly turn to the disadvantage of contemporary decorators. How can they stand, the poor souls, the comparison of their production with the masterpieces of past centuries? It is not a fair match. It has little to do with the legitimacy of their courageous attempts at originality, although that is the crux of the matter. They are overwhelmed by the weight of the consecrated glory of their predecessors. These are not very equitable proceedings, within the means of minor judges, and so terribly easy. During the literary battles of the 18th century, when our French authors, Corneille, Racine or Molière pitted against the Greek and Latin classics were not treated worsely than our unfortunate ornamentists in respect to their illustrious ancestors Berain, Caffieri, Boulle, Crescent or Germain. That is the usual aspect of those types of discussions, which, in any case, go nowhere and prove nothing.

Since last year at the Universal Exhibition where a certain number of French and foreign decorative works exemplifying an incontestably new spirit were brought together, the very basis of these innovations has started to be denounced with surprising force. Mischevious critiques were added to more serious ones to crush with their sarcasm these audacious artists who dared to attempt to be no longer dull copiers and provide current society with furniture conceived after their manner. With what cruel irony their experiments were judged! With what pitiless and meticulous severity their furniture, gold and silver crafts, and jewelry were analyzed and described. The distinguished writer Robert de La Sizeranne showed himself to be particularly harsh concerning them in the *Revue des Deux Mondes*. Afterward, the jolly crowd of pamphleteers vied with each other in sharpening their epigrammes. Nowadays it is good form to seem to reprove the tendancies of Art Nouveau, while affecting to have noticed only the exaggerations, faults and absurdities. One must call it "whip lash", "laniers", "rabbit guts" or "mutton bone" art, alluding to certain forms dear to some of the avant-garde artists. "Modern style" is pronounced with an English accent, with infinite disdain, and is used as an adjective to sum up all the incommensurable pity that this original art effort, outside of pastiches and the conventional, excites in a certain category of amateurs. These expressions have even been replaced by the epithet "fin de siècle". To characterize someone who stands out by his way of thinking, his haircut or the shape of his hat, it is said "He's a *modern style*". That, in itself, is not really mean.

This state of mind – which manifests the eternal resistance of the past to the present and that of good sense to the extremists of a just doctrine – is relayed constantly in newspapers, books and speeches. Quite recently the magazine *Le Temps* published a column by Frump bubbling with wit which exploded like a flare in the Art Nouveau camp, deriding its conceptions of furniture and ornament. The thing is entitled "A Crisis of Artistism". The author portrays a "sportsman" who, through a chance invitation, ends up in a house where, to his inconvenience, the eccentricities of Modern Style prevail from top to bottom and in excess. In the antechamber, our man finds himself face to face with a disturbing coatrack.

"This piece, he said, forebode much pain for me. It was, as it stood, of tortuous form and the copper pegs represented the elongated bodies of virgins. I hesitated hanging my hat on such thinness, but the salon door was already opened and the servant was announcing me."

Here the guest enters the salon where the hostess reclining on a bookcase received him.

"What, on a bookcase?"

"I mean on a fireplace, in short, on a composite, bizarre piece of furniture. Imagine a divan surmounted by a shelf overflowing with books up against the ledge of a fireplace where ceramic pots were grouped. She did not rise to welcome me, wishing to appear in the carefully arranged surroundings which had been prepared to charm me... She was veiled in anæmic fabrics on which morbid flowers were dimly visible... As she talked, I examined with curiosity the rings which weighted down her fingers... I could hardly make out those pretentious jeweller's compositions. I could distinguish a contorted body, a flexing monster, a grimacing faun and an agitated virgin. All the imaginative forces of the young poets of yesterday, or rather the day before yesterday, were reaffirmed here in precious materials. Madame Norbert's two hands were an anthology of the symbolist school."

He goes upstairs to his room and there he finds furniture which meets the descriptions of certain works seen in our annual exhibitions.

"I began to shudder right away as I looked around me with terror. The paper covering the walls was a lost, desperate battle of tapeworms and I knew that horrible dreams were going to haunt me. The panels of the bed were all sculpted and a circle of witches was madly spinning. A small shelf completed the piece and I was tormented by the idea that, if I moved too much in my sleep, all the iridescent glasspieces placed there by a delicate hand would come crashing down on my nose. The wardrobe was decorated with iron mountings on which menacing sergeants stood guard. The idea of advancing my fingers to open the door was an unbearable thought. Despondent, I sought a seat to fall down on to reflect on my sad state but the chairs and armchairs were all crouching monsters and I could not bring myself to sit on their heads. I went to the bathroom and I wanted to plunge my head under water to clear my thinking. In the wash basin, my dear friend, a sonnet was inscribed in the wash basin!"

The dining room was no less a surprise but what was the most remarkable was the ladies'jewelry.

In generously low-necked dresses, (although some of them were obviously too thin for such a show), they wore necklaces which ressembled iron collars and chains at the end of which hung pendants which looked like plumb-bobs. These strange jewels brought to mind classical references: in them were hidden numerous stories, as many as were engraved on the shields of the soldiers who fought in the Trojan War. The clasps of the necklaces displayed shepherds playing the flute under tall trees in a forest, while a nymph fled to a nearby grotto; desperate, shivering princesses in front of terrifying monsters; women struggling against attacking frogs, powerful men fighting in hand to hand combat. The pendants revealed swans gliding on the water, the embrace of the knight and the maiden under fully-bloomed thistles, pious bowing in front of Byzantine idols, Ophelias with flowing locks, advancing towards death...

In short, there was so much art everywhere in this Modern Style house. The slightest ustensil is so loaded down with curious ornamentation, elevating it so far above its role that the hero of this adventure has only one thing in mind: to flee and to regard objects of rustic simplicity. After this trial, nothing appears more beautiful to him than his trunk, his modest trunk with solid wooden panels, happily devoid of any carving.

Such caricatures, however witty they might be, could in no way stop the inventive momentum of our contemporary decorators, nor hinder the movement which is henceforth irresistible, pushing our society to want furniture which is truly appropriate to its use, and not copied on that of the wealthy lords of the Louis XIV period, whose needs were quite different from ours. Nothing is more normal, more legitimate than this desire. Shall we say that the terms "Art Nouveau" and "Modern Style" have the fault of being too ambitious, because they have applied only in fact, until now, to simple experiments? Agreed! This objection is childish, but it is enough to agree on the value of these expressions. Let us not haggle over terms and exaggerate their significance.

Is there not something that our artists, infatuated with innovation, should retain from the jokes which their efforts provoke?

The orientation of modern art

Charles Genuys, professor at the Ecole nationale des arts décoratifs, in *La Revue des Arts décoratifs*, Paris, 1901, vol. I pp. 3-5.

The wheels are in motion: it is essential for it now not to lose impetus.

If art in the making, while jealously preserving its formulas, does not impose on itself some of the guidelines which previous styles observed throughout time, if it does not prune the eccentricities of its lone, boisterous fantasy, its future could prove uncertain.

Without assuming a somewhat unfashionable dogmatic attitude, it is possible to say that, if this art is to survive and develop, it must, just like its respected ancestors from Antiquity and the Middle Ages, stay within the limits of absolute logic concerning use of materials and suitability to the imposed needs, while remaining clearly interesting, varied and expressive.

In practice the application of these few principles can be summarized as follows:

Do not claim that buildings must be destroyed and libraries burned down, that is to say return to primitive, savage times, under the pretext that stocking documents hinders the development of the imagination. Being primitive is not within everyone's grasp. Secondly, experience has proven that this hindrance is only relative; it in no way disturbs freedom nor does it prevent deviations. The best way is to be well-acquainted with the past, all the pasts, to determine their principles and to appropriate that which should be retained.

Respect for the rules of logic will lead to a modification, in the rational sense, of forms which cannot be built, or built only poorly. Each assembly of wood, stone or iron will be carefully thought through and established. How many pieces of so-called modern furniture can keep their initial make-up if they are only the consequence of undisciplined fantasy?

The same principle of logic, regarding suitability to purpose, will determine the proper layout of a building as well as the most simple chair.

Penetrating the secrets of the comfort of 18th century chairs and taking avantage of their popularity can be useful.

As to the expressive role of modern art, it will depend as much on the artist who creates as on the environment in which he evolves. There is a question of time period: it is essential that the artist warrant his title, that he do away with the insignificant and commonplace and that he express his own personality.

The interpretation of nature is often advised as the only source of sound invention. Although it is not novel, it is in fact excellent advice. It arises from an understandable admiration for ornamentation on monuments from the Middle Ages and the already established theories of Viollet-le-Duc and Ruprich-Robert.

However, one should ask of nature only what it can provide, that is to say, details and not complete entities. The Paris Opera or Cathedral could never be conceived from a horse chestnut leaf, but a judicious choice of plants, animals and figures can add interesting and captivating character to the decoration of the building for both the eye and the mind.

The combination of lines framing the form, their selection, their straightness, their delicate or robust curves, if they are created by true artists, are nonetheless, in spite of and perhaps because of their abstact nature, the simplest and most noble mode of expression.

Here once again be aware of hastily formed opinions and prevailing ideas.

Within these slightly annoying limits, which are as far removed from a narrow doctrine as they are from reckless abandon without guidelines, modern art can survive and develop, without titles, epithets, freed from prejudicial tares. The gigantic, generous effort of the 1900 Universal Exhibition will not have been in vain.

To contribute in this same direction and with measure to the ongoing evolution: that is the role a journal like ours can play.

Illuminate the present in the light of the past, show the path to follow while indicating vigilantly the obstacles to avoid, bring together all the free spirits, open-minded talents, artists of good will, in a joint effort against routine. That is a sound undertaking, a necessary task.

Better still! Above all, order has to be restored in the minds which have been troubled both by those who exclusively espouse ancient art and by the audacious who, in the pursuit of novelty, have courted incoherence and nonsense.

Too many snobs in France welcome graceless foreign models which are in contradiction with the spirit of our race. It is time, even past the time, to react. Let us go forward yet hold onto our own identity.

On style, tradition and nature

Concerning imitation and tradition, the problem appears complicated and it indeed is so, due to the public who call for manufacturers who do not argue and artists who obey in order to earn a living. What is wanted is work done nowadays that resembles work done in the past. Whether the object is in the medieval, Renaissance or Louis XV style, the craftsman is always invited to a repetition. He thus repeats, and most often poorly for lack of good models. He does not consult the originals because these originals are not at his disposal and it is unfortunate since he would probably learn things which he did not know; he would learn about proportions, robustness, construction, a type of "soundness" which is quickly disappearing. All he finds in his model books are approximations furnishing only relative ideas of the originals which were designated as examples. He copies these impressions and we know what great number of vacuous, inexact pieces are produced by these methods. I was going to say that I was not only speaking of craftsmen subject to industrial production, but who is not subject to this? There are sculptors to be excluded here, who have entered the race and who imagine and produce unique pieces, worthy of notice, but they are not germane to the present discussion. I am, therefore, speaking of the interesting group of craftsmen who trained in art schools or served as apprentices. I notice that they all have the same disorder, the same powerlessness, from the most humble to the most well-renown.

It is among them, I believe, that it would be good to introduce the idea that to understand tradition well, one must comprehend the meaning of the lesson of nature and return to the organic. The combinations, forms, directions and differences in nature are unlimited. Ask nature its secrets, as those before you have done, and know how to understand them. Think of the infinite variety of aspects to be found in stones, seashells, plants and animals of all kinds. Within this lively jumble, seek out what is suitable to your way of thinking and your manual work. You will not copy because, however hard you try, it is impossible to copy. You will adapt existing forms to your intended purposes. Scrupulous care will lead you slowly through imperceptible stages toward creations springing from your imagination. Do not worry about whether you are redoing things which have already been done. All you need do is to place yourself in front of present forms. All you need accomplish is to distinguish yourself from your predecessors by a single detail. You will easily find this detail if you are patient and sincere, if you do not pretend to change Art, if you are humble and fervent before the innumerable and inexhaustible riches that the universe has to offer.

Gustave Geoffroy in *La Revue des Arts décoratifs*, Paris 1898, vol. II, pp. 180-181.

THE ART MARKET

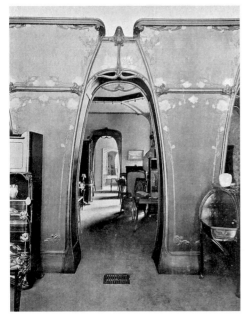

Jansen Shop, rue Royale, Paris. Interior design by Henri Sauvage. Furniture by Louis Majorelle.

A first Art Nouveau style was organized by independant artists incapable of profitting from a production studio; their experimentation was regularly commented by art journals, or even the general press on occasion like the Salon National des Beaux-Arts. Another Art Nouveau style was in the hands of medium-sized companies in cabinet-making, glassmaking and art foundries. Their strength reposed on their own design studios in charge of creating models; their financial and material organization allowed them to sell large quantities of products by catalogue on the national and international markets.

The first of these two adhered to the rules of the art market. It was fragile and allergic to the most minor crisis. The second could affront disaffectation, if it were short-lived. The two were made to co-exist. This alliance culminated in France at the 1900 Universal Exhibition and continued until the Decorative Arts Exhibition in Torino in 1902. It then had to give way to the growing success of German and Austrian industries which in turn were arousing curiosity. Although activity was maintained and despite the growth of houses like Daum and Majorelle, the laboratory of French Art Nouveau was only the shadow of its former self. In 1904 two famous private galleries in Paris closed their doors: *Maison Moderne*, managed by Jules Meier-Graefe since 1899, and *Salon de l'Art Nouveau*, managed by Samuel Bing; a year earlier *Maison d'Art Lorraine* in Nancy, directed by Charles Fridrich, had also closed.

Everything, however, had begun auspiciously for Samuel Bing, the most publicized gallery owner of the movement. When he arrived from Hamburg in 1871, he first set up shop in the ceramics business and importing Japanese objects. After a fact-finding trip to the United States entrusted to him by the administrative director of the Ecole des Beaux-Arts and a trip to Brussels where he visited Edmond Picard's *Maison d'Art* store, he seemed convinced that French industry lacked artists "devoted fully to crafts". When he opened the *Salon de l'Art Nouveau* at 22, rue de Provence on December 26, 1895, next to his Japanese art gallery, and organized periodic exhibitions at the new address,

Bing stirred up interest among a well-informed public composed of collectors, artists, journalists and amateurs. Designed by Parisian architect Louis Bonnier, decorated with a frieze on the façade by the Belgian Frank Brangwyn, this gallery welcomed a selection of works by French and foreign artists for its first exhibit. Works on show were notably by Anquetin, Besnard, Conder, Cross, Guillaumin, Lemmen, Luce, Pissarro, Ranson, Signac, Toulouse-Lautrec, Vuillard and Van Rysselberghe with drawings by Aubrey Bearsdley and sculptures by Bourdelle, Charpentier, Constantin Meunier and Rodin. Also exhibited were ceramics by Bigot, Dalpayrat, Dammouse, Delaherche, works of glass by Cros, Gallé, Tiffany, jewelry by Lalique, a bedroom suite designed by Maurice Denis; a dining room, smoking room, a collector's cabinet and a rotunda by Henry Van de Velde. On display was a suite of stained glass after cartoons by Bonnard, Denis, Grasset, Roussel, Toulouse-Lautrec, Vallotton and Vuillard brought together by Tiffany's of New York. One-man shows by Constantin Meunier, Eugène Carrière and Edvard Munch followed. When Bing became a manufacturer in 1899 in order to prepare the Universal Exhibition the following year, design, sculpture, cabinet-making and jewelry studios were established. For the same reason, he encouraged Georges van Slüyters (called Georges de Feure), Edouard Colonna and Eugène Gaillard to work as decorators.

It must be mentioned that this bevy of artists assembled by Bing did not presuppose a real creed. In his memoirs Van de Velde noted how out of place he felt in this strange group which Bing had brought together; composed of artists who wanted to do something new and sell their works. But Bing had never sought to create intellectual dynamics within the group. Juxtaposing furniture by the Belgian artist whose desire was to simplify form with those by Maurice Denis and Rubert Carabin could do nothing to clarify the objectives of the movement.

Louis Bonnier. *Le Salon de l'Art Nouveau*, rue de Provence in Paris.
Institut Français d'Architecture, Paris.

Anonymous. Excerpt from *Ornements sur l'art industriel au vingtième siècle (Collection of some of the main works of the collaborators of La Maison Moderne)*, Paris, 1901.

La Maison Moderne

Henry Van de Velde. Interior design of *La Maison Moderne*, rue des Petits-Champs, Paris.

One of the most envious titles of modern criticism in the esteem of posterity will be to have "established the social mission of Art and revealed the possibility of a more gentle destiny, one which is better for man because it confers dignified adornment on all the corners of his life". In every country, minds steeped in philosophy have spared no energy to promote the beneficial exercise of æsthetic sensitivity and to ask "that nothing be proposed to our sight, to our use, that Art has not ennobled by the prestige of beauty".

Today we see the effect of these demands and how we are in their debt for the renaissance of the industries of peace and the home. Mr Meier-Graefe is one of among the initiators of this movement, and the role he undertook was both very essential and very special.

Ten years ago, it was his pleasure to support in the journals, and with the warmth of an impassioned soul, the doctrine of equality within the arts. He even succeeded in rallying the most precious supporters to his cause, but Mr Meier-Graefe did not content himself with the contemplative and usually inefficient action of the critics. He went about proving what he had written, moved on from theory to practice, from propaganda to facts. The origin of the creation of *Maison Moderne* is none other than a firmly-established desire to satisfy an ideal which William Morris shared, among our friends on the other side of the Channel, and in which no one on our side had succeeded until 1898.

The purpose of this new founding was not to add another exhibition gallery of paintings and statues to the numerous ones already in existence, but to form a fraternal association of the arts and especially to rejuvenate the useful, applied arts and bring them to meet present needs. There is no prouder undertaking, but also none more difficult to bring to a successful conclusion. The painter or the sculptor does not encounter obstacles concerning materials in the expression of his ideas. To formulate them, a bit of canvas, a block of clay suffice. He is inventor and executant, for all the parts, at every instant, the master of the work. This is far removed from the decorator's plight. To become viable, to be incarnated in a solid definitive material, his concept demands the assistance of a craft, of a factory. […]

Firstly, poorly informed of the traditions and laws of his craft, the painter or the sculptor delighted in more or less strange inventions, but which were devoid of practical adaptations or possible use. Some architects manifested great concern for the needs of function but lacked knowledge concerning the building preferences of the race. For an instant, a British or Flemish influence almost predominated. The unexpected was desired at all costs, without delay, even if it entailed an abrupt break with the past. The purpose, however, was in no way to shame tradition but "to pursue it while renewing it". It was only after the period of obscurantism, of trial and error, were over, and after having benefitted from the initial experiences, that *Maison Moderne* began to propose the necessary solutions to the problem of Art Nouveau. Its essential principle is to assert itself above all as being French and only to accept those foreign inventions which were produced in agreement with our national spirit or which could promote its development through rational, free assimilation. As regards its program, it has remained exactly what Mr. Meier-Graefe set out in his writings when he beseeched art to embellish life and to create a harmonious setting for it.

It is the entire decor of our lives that should be adapted to the trends of taste and modern spirit. The aspect of everthing in the home needed to be changed, recreated: domestic and ornamental objects, furniture, wallhangings, rugs, lighting fixtures, tableware, glassware, as well as marble, metal, enamel and ceramic products. The choice of these objects reflects our individuality; they are the witnesses and confidants of our acts and daily gestures. Even women's jewelry would covet being set free and emancipated.

The Houses of Art

Emile Nicolas, "Les Maisons d'Art" in *La Lorraine Artiste*, January 15, 1901, pp. 120-121.

The major industries, through high production levels, utilize conventional commercial means to distribute and sell their wares in different cities throughout France and abroad. The solitary artist, on the other hand, cannot profit from these advantages. He has neither the time nor the competency nor the means to find outlets for his production. Hence, he often remains unknown to his fellow citizens and obliged to abandon a craft which could be lucrative, but he also has the immense advantage of leaving him the owner of his talent and permits him not to be "reduced to the state of a machine" nor force him "to execute by the sweat of his brow pieces of the works of others, without being able to to embrace the entire work" as Mr Emile Gallé expresses it so eloquently.

To prevent this regrettable state of affairs, the idea of establishing Houses of Art was adopted to offer the best reception of works by all craftsmen, especially those by the most modest ones. By centralizing the production scattered throughout a city or a region into one store was the only way to permit each craftsman to sell his work.

It was not without a certain apprehension that the great industrialists and specialized merchants faced this quite modern undertaking. Very eager to conserve their prestige, and also probably their clientele, they voiced their opposition to the Houses of Art. This is quite human, but they can rest assured; we are convinced they will not lose a single customer and to the contrary, it is to their advantage that these Houses prosper because they play a pedagogical role of prime importance. We can not hide the fact that modern art has not been completely accepted and many people still deny its existence.

Since the Houses of Art are open to all, they attract the curious who, without knowing it, educate their eye and their mind through constant contact with new forms. The Houses train the public's taste and contribute to the disappearance of prejudices that most people still harbor against the new ideas of decoration.

Better than a museum, they are constantly replenishing the works they exhibit, works produced by local artists and also those from others parts of France and abroad, giving us the opportunity to judge the work and trends of our competitors. Finally, they can encourage the young by organizing contests and awarding prizes to the best entries. In a word, they are active organizations and, better than the best organized company, they contribute daily to advancing artists and the public along the road of artistic progress.

Henri Bergé. Poster for *La Maison d'Art Lorraine*, 1900.

The inauguration of the Salon of Art Nouveau

Henry van de Velde in *Récit de ma vie.*

The inauguration of the exhibition took place during the last days of December. It was a sensational event. Elegant and select, noisy, hostile and indignant, the throng pressed forward. The cream of Paris society, the most renown art critics, numerous celebrities from the artistic circles were manifestly just as offended as the throng, although they remained reserved in deference to Samuel Bing's highly esteemed reputation. He appeared to be the victim of a deplorable and unutterable adventure which might cost him the prestige he had enjoyed heretofore as the most infallible connoisseur and taste arbiter.

Outside, in the street, in front of the façade by the architect Bonnier which caused such an uproar, – he is one of the nicest and best men I have ever met – the visitors, who had been uncontrollable during the exhibition, seemed to calm down. Groups formed around the most well-known personalities. Dignified gentleman that he is, Edmond de Goncourt waited until he was outside to throw up his hands. He was, however, the sole person with enough imagination to see the relationship between my furniture and the design of yachts and competition sailboats. He christened my style "the yacht style". De Goncourt was close to the true definition: to illustrate my design principles, he chose one of the most striking examples of rational design and functional forms. At that time, it was almost exclusively in naval construction, coach-building and in several other industries of domestic objects that the tradition of rational design continued to exist. Rodin came to his aid by uttering insults in regards to Meier-Graefe. Rodin could not help but recognize his role in the disavowal of Bing's attachment to French tradition and his rallying to the most odious form of internationalism. "Your van de Velde", Rodin yelled as the crowd applauded him, "Your van de Velde is a barbarian!"

The epithet which the indignant Rodin used to express the impact that my furniture had had on him was only inappropriate because the great sculptor had meant it in a pejorative sense. I had designed them as a barbarian, that is in the manner of Byzantine and Gothic craftsmen who went to the one and only source of rational design while seeking to adapt form to function. Who better than Rodin, a passionate amateur of cathedrals to recognize this link, however distant and modest it might be?

However, inside his gallery, Bing, who had counted on a completely different reception, was visibly shaken. He tried to clutch on to someone or something, and as he shook our hands convulsively, he murmured, "Besnard and you, van de Velde, you saved me!". In fact, there could be no talk of a rescue; the outcome of the battle was more than overwhelming. The top critics and the editors of the important newspapers showed little consideration for Samuel Bing. Octave Mirbeau and Arsène Alexandre, beside themselves with indignation, spoke disparagingly and peevishly about the exhibition. Mourey took refuge behind a wait-and-see attitude. Only Camille Mauclair of *La Renaissance* journal, Geffroy from the *Journal*, and Thadée Natanson from *La Revue blanche* were kindly disposed and sympathetic.

Naturalist School against Modern Style

We preached in the workshops for the renewal of furniture through the use of nature. But many of those who consider themselves modern have held onto a limited number of conventional themes. Their furniture is a combination of purely geometrical cabinets, and not of living concepts based on the observation of organic structure. Mind you, in Schools whichever they may be, static construction had to be reckoned with before considering the decorative covering of the piece. Quite frequently nowadays, one must admit, the men who consider themselves innovaters are only copiers of the originators whom they have poorly comprehended and overlook construction and practicality absolutely. They lapse into the bizarre. And, a very curious thing worthy of notice, they are the very ones who accumulate the worst eccentricities of the most artificial type of decoration. It is they who take finery and opulence for what is actually dearth and affectation.

Emile Gallé in "Le Mobilier contemporain orné d'après la nature", *La Lorraine*, Nancy, January 1, 1900, pp. 34-35.

On the other hand, nature, – this might come to you as a surprise – which does not furnish festoons and astragals, does however provide much more than earthworms and tapeworms, pseudo-kelp and panic-stricken vermicelli. With these, albeit executed with great talent, they wanted to make, a helminthic, larval style cradle for 1900 in which to agitate the 20th century. If that is modern furniture, we consent to donning wigs and tail coats.

But fortunately, there is another style available, which is based on principles and not excesses. What are these principles?

1. A piece of furniture is made for use, a chair is not created to be exhibited among Mr Alfred Picard's international agglomerations of phenomena. It is made to procure rest and a stable sitting position for people with loins, legs and a back. It must provide all that and be sufficiently solid.

A bed is not assembled to give hospitality day and night to vases by Mr Bigot and books bound by Mr Pertus Ruban. It is not indispensable to be able to climb up and sit on top of a sideboard, or that a cupboard be flanked with applied art on both sides: on the right, a night side and on the left, the gnarled outgrowth of a coocoo clock. It is not absolutely necessary either for Madame to give the impression that she is receiving company in a dining-car, a harem or in the *Chat Noir Inn*, nor do the backs of our light ball chairs, called "fly-ing chairs", take off to the ceiling as in the *Pilules du Diable* play, nor do the armchairs in a reception room need be soldered to the fireplace or be an integral part of the building.

These singularities have nothing to do with utility. It is a tentacular, teratological style.

2. Construction must correspond to the function of the work and the materials used. Construction must also be as simple, as logical as possible.

3. This sound construction must be apparent and not be concealed in any manner.

4. Now we arrive at the decoration of the work.

Decoration includes:

1. The curves of framing: columns, stays, joists, feet and arms of armchairs: in a word, the structure.

2. The pieces of superficial ornamentation which are added to the work to underline details, function and special embellishments.

Concerning the forms of the framing, the best are those chosen from known shapes, which are more or less always the same, or to use flora and possibly fauna as a source of inspiration.

These last two sources, and especially the use of plants, are the only ones we recommend for furniture.

The forms provided by plants are naturally adaptable to wood. They are of infinite beauty and variety. Plants are naturally adorned by the characteristic structures of the varied organs during their growth cycle. Among the innumerable plant families, genus and species, each possesses its own general and particular style.

Art Nouveau

O. Mirbeau in *Le Journal*, December 22, 1901.

During one of my moody strolls, I met the alert and triumphant, joyful-eyed Mr. C... Mr C is one of the promoters in France of Art Nouveau, of that abominable and caricatural art, which is not art and which is not new. He has carried his proselytizing to the point of becoming, from the rich collector and curious amateur he was, an active popularizer and producer.

He has opened a store in the center of Paris where all these horrors are on display.

"Well" he said to me, "It is going well!.. It is going well! We are triumphant!"

"Alas!"

He showed a look of disdain. "It's true," he continued, "You, you do not believe in progress! You are aloof from progress! You stay behind the times... in the Louis XVI, I wager..."

He did not give me time to respond... Besides, what use was there to respond?

"Oh! Louis XVI!"... he continued, shrugging his shoulders. "Well!.. for me... as time passes... the more I find that beastly... idiotic... hideous!.. Look, I have gotten to the point... I am not talking about owning... looking... looking, do you understand, at a Louis XVI fabric... I find that revolting... That throws me into such a rage... that it takes me several days to get over it!.. The purity, simplicity, harmony and grace of Louis XVI style!.. Oh! Permit me to laugh!.. Oh! no! I am no longer to be taken in!.. I am a man of my times, Heavens!.. a modern man! And what if the Louis XVI is beautiful, what can that change for a man of progress... for the man of the present that I am? Is is past... it is finished... Ugly modern is worth a thousand times the old beautiful!.. And it is so true that... Look... here is what happened to me... The other day, I found a Louis XVI coffee-pot at my house... a Louis XVI coffee-pot, at my house!.. at my house!.. Do you understand me? It is mad!.. I thought I was going to be ill... I gave it to my cook..."

"The illness?"

"No, the coffee-pot. Well! My cook did not want it... She refused it indignantly... She told me, 'A Louis XVI coffee-pot... Oh! Sir, I never would have thought it possible from you, Sir'. It is obvious!.. Even common people, my dear gentleman!.. Oh, It is going well... It is going well!.. Have you seen my exhibition?"

"No... not yet..."

"You must see it, my dear sir... By Jove!.. It is very important!.. I have a coffee-pot in my exhibition. Yes... but a Louis XVI coffee-pot. Oh! No!.. a modern coffee-pot... It is galvanized cow-dung... and it represents... a Roquefort cheese... That, that is a coffee-pot. Well then, have you seen my clock?"

"No."

"But good Lord! Have you seen nothing? My clock is wonderful!.. The dial, a sunflower, in blue copper..."

"Blue?"

"But of course!.. Yellow copper or red copper, what progress!.. I who am of the present... I think that copper should be blue!"

And he continued the description of his clock. "The pendulum is the stem of the flower... It looks like a stem beaten down by a heavy wind... For, in art, the beauty of the form is not all, there must be movement... For the base, I think I have found something quite ingenious. In general, on what does a plant rest? On roots, no? Well! The base of my clock, they are the roots of the sunflower, bur roots which are so twisted, entangled, involved that they are like the intestines of a man ill with infectious enteritis... It is superb!"

And as he walked, more and more enthusiastically, he told me, "A chair – it is a tree!.. An armchair – it is a guinea fowl... A wardrobe, it is a fireplace... A fireplace, it is a chest of drawers. It is obvious... it is obvious... Ask Granet, de Feure, Armand Point!"

As he left me, he was still saying, "We did not achieve perfection right away. A style is not

invented... like that... in one day... No, Good Lord! We groped along... I agree... We hesitated... And then... the habit of old forms... known lines... all that heredity of antiquated things... Oh! it is not always easy, my dear gentleman... For example for an armchair... Try as we could, the back became the feet and the feet, the back... well... it was not exactly right... There was still the seat... What to do with the seat. Do away with it? Turn it around? Well then what?.. Oh! the beginnings were very difficult, I admit it... But by dint of breaking lines and deforming forms, we finally achieved something really new... completely original... Hence, I assure you, I have found the definitive modern style, the 20th century style... Please come and see it. You will be astonished!.. Word of honor!.. Good day!"

Two days later, I went to Mr. C's home. He showed me a Louis XVI couch and two armchairs, in the most pure Louis XVI style.

"What?"... he said as he glanced at me out of the corner of his eye, with an expression which was both triumphant and malicious, "Definitive, no? Pretty? You think so?"

By dint of breaking lines and reconstituting them, he had ended up, he, the man of his times, by inventing the Louis XVI.

I left without bothering to disenchant him.

And to what use? He would have, the next day, invented the Louis XV... and perhaps even the Gothic!..

BIBLIOGRAPHY

Art Nouveau in France:
BRUNHAMMER Y. and al. *Art Nouveau Belgium France*, Institute for the Arts Rice University, and The Art Institute of Chicago, 1976.
SILVERMAN D. L. *L'Art Nouveau en France; politique, psychologie et style fin de siècle*, Flammarion, Paris, 1994.

Art Nouveau in Nancy:
Art Nouveau, l'École de Nancy, Denoël et Serpenoise, Paris et Nancy, 1987.
Fleurs et Ornements, Réunion des Musées Nationaux, Paris, 1999.
L'École de Nancy, 1889-1909, Art Nouveau et industries d'art, Réunion des Musées Nationaux, Paris, 1999.
MIDANT J.-P., WEISBERG G. et SALMON B. *Peinture et Art Nouveau*, Réunion des Musées Nationaux, Paris, 1999.
Nancy 1900, Rayonnement de l'Art Nouveau, Klopp, Thionville, 1989.
DANIEL-WIESER F. *Les Dames de Nancy*, La Nuée Bleue, Éditions de l'Est, Strasbourg, 1998.
DEBIZE C. *Émile Gallé l'École de Nancy*, Serpenoise, Metz, 1998.
DEBIZE C. *Guide de l'École de Nancy,* Presses Universitaire de Nancy, Serpenoise, Metz.
DUSART A. et MOULIN F. *Art Nouveau. L'épopée Lorraine*, La Nuée Bleue, Éditions de l'Est, Strasbourg, 1998.

Art Nouveau in Paris:
BORSI F. *Paris 1900*, Marc Vokaer, Bruxelles.
De l'impressionnisme à l'Art Nouveau, Réunion des Musées Nationaux, Paris, 1996.
Paris-Bruxelles, Réunion des Musées Nationaux, Paris, 1997.
TSCHUDI MADSEN S. *L'Art Nouveau*, Hachette, Paris, 1967.

1. Emile Gallé
CHARPENTIER F. T. *Emile Gallé, industriel et poète*, Presses Universitaires de Nancy, Nancy, 1978.
CHARPENTIER F. T. and THIÉBAULT P. *Gallé*, Paris, 1985.
GALLE E. *Ecrits sur l'art*, Éditions Jeanne Lafitte, Marseille, 1998.
LE TACON F. *Emile Gallé ou le Mariage de l'Art et de la Science*, Messene et Jean de Cousance, Paris, 1995.
LE TACON F. *L'Œuvre de verre d'Emile Gallé*, Messene et Jean de Cousance, Paris, 1998.
THIÉBAULT P. *Les Dessins de Gallé*, Réunion des Musées Nationaux, Paris, 1993.

2. Eugène Grasset
MURRAY-ROBERTSON A. *Eugène Grasset, pionnier de l'Art Nouveau*, éditions 24 heures, Lausanne, 1981.

3. Hector Guimard
FRONTISI C. *Guimard Hector, Architectures*, les amis d'Hector Guimard, Paris, sd.
Hector Guimard, Academy editions – Denoël, Paris, 1978.
Guimard, Réunion des Musées Nationaux, Paris, 1992.
GUIMARD H. *Actes du colloque international organisé par le musée d'Orsay*, Réunion des Musées de France, Paris, 1994.

4. Victor Prouvé
PROUVÉ M. *Victor Prouvé*, Berger-Levrault, Nancy, 1958.

5. The plant
MIDANT J.-P. *Sèvres 1900*, Musée des Beaux-Arts, Nancy, 1996.

6. Water
COLLECTIF. *Autour de Lévy-Dhurmer. Visionnaires et intimistes en 1900*, Grand Palais, Paris, 1973.

7. The cycle of life

BAJOU V. *Eugène Carrière*, éditions Acatos, Lausanne, 1998.

MAUCLAIR C. *Albert Besnard*, Librairie Delagrave, Paris, 1914.

8. Woman

ELLRIDGE A. *Mucha*, Terrail, Paris, 1992.

François-Rupert Carabin 1862-1932, Musées de Strasbourg, 1993.

Georges de Feure: du symbolisme à l'Art Nouveau (1890-1905), Musée du Prieuré, Saint-Germain-en-Laye, 1995.

9. Dance

LISTA G. *Loïe Fuller danseuse de la Belle Époque*, Stock-Somogy éditions d'art, Paris, 1994.

10. Works as perpetual training

De Carpeaux à Matisse, Édition de l'Association des Conservateurs de la Région Nord-Pas-de-Calais, Lille, 1982.

La Sculpture française au XIXe siècle, Réunion des Musées Nationaux, Paris, 1986.

Regards. Collection du musée des Beaux-Arts de Nancy, Réunion des Musées Nationaux, Paris, 1999.

11. The home

BASCOU M. "Une boiserie Art Nouveau d'Alexandre Charpentier", *Revue du Louvre*, Paris, 1979, n°3, p. 219.

BOUVIER R. *Majorelle, une aventure moderne*, La Bibliothèque des Arts, Serpenoise, Metz, 1991.

DESCOUTURELLE F. *Eugène Vallin*, Nancy, 1999.

PÉTRY C. et al. *Daum dans les musées de Nancy*, Nancy, 1989.

12. Modern houses and apartment building

BARRÉ-DESPOND A. *Frantz Jourdain*, éditions du Regard, Paris, 1988.

Henri Sauvage, éditions A.A.M., Bruxelles, 1976.

MARREY B. *Louis Bonnier*, Mardaga, Liège, 1988.

Nancy 1900, Inventaire général des richesses artistiques de la France, Nancy, 1998.

VIGATO J.-C. *L'École de Nancy et la Question architecturale*, Messene, Paris, 1998.

13. Shops and restaurants

"Architecture et Gastronomie", *Monuments historiques*, Paris, février-mars 1984, n°131.

14. The Universal Exposition

Le Livre des Expositions Universelles, Union Centrale des Arts Décoratifs, Paris, 1983.

15. The art market

Documents sur l'art industriel au XXe siècle, édition de la Maison Moderne, Paris, 1901.

WATELET J. G. *Serrurier-Bovy*, Atelier Vokaer – CFC, Bruxelles, 1986.

WEISBERG G. P. *Art Nouveau Bing; Paris Style 1900*, New York, Harry N. Abrams publishers in association with the Smithsonian Institution traveling exhibition service, Washington DC, 1986.

Contents

Printed in Italy